CLEVELAND LANDMARKS SERIES
VOLUME II

# CLEVELAND MUNICIPAL STADIUM

## BY JIM TOMAN & DAN COOK

# Publishing Information



Printed in the United States of America

ISBN — 0-936760-02-8

Library of Congress Catalog Card Number 81-65716

Published By:

Cleveland Landmarks Press, Inc.
P.O. Box 9152
Cleveland, Ohio 44137

FIRST PRINTING

OTHER BOOKS IN THIS SERIES:

*The Terminal Tower Complex, Volume I*

Cleveland Landmarks Series
Tom Luckay, Editor

# Acknowledgements

There are many to whom the authors are indebted for their help and support during the writing of this volume. Without their cooperation this venture could not have been completed. To all of them — many thanks.

At the head of the list is Art Modell, Stadium Corporation president, whose co-operation made this project feasible. He extended to the authors the amenities of the Stadium and its staff, and provided support for the undertaking.

The authors are grateful to Stadium staffers Mike Poplar, Pete Pucher, and Bob Boylan, who all gave freely of their time. And in a very special way, thanks goes to Dino Lucarelli, whose guiding hand and wise counsel greatly facilitated this venture. At every step of the way, Dino was there with encouragement, insight, and assistance.

The authors are also indebted: to Nate Wallack of the Cleveland Browns; to Gabe Paul and Rosemary (Posie) O'Conner of the Cleveland Indians; and to Marshall Bossard of the Indians' ground crew.

Gratitude is expressed to the many staffers of The Cleveland **Press** who were very helpful: Herb Kamm, Bob Love, Bob August, Tom Barensfeld, Bob Noyes, and Fred Sockol. In difficult times for them, they did not hesitate to take time from their busy schedules to assist the authors in their research efforts.

The authors are also indebted to Grace Parch, Pat McCarty and Joe Seminic of The **Plain Dealer;** to Ed Barmann of the **Catholic Universe Bulletin;** to Jim Harper of the Osborne Engineering Company; to the dedicated librarians and staffers of the Cleveland Public Library and the Cuyahoga County Library who helped in finding so many pieces of isolated information, and to Commissioner Frank Duman of the City of Cleveland for his insights and support.

Also of real help, as before, were Series Editor Tom Luckay; Brian Azzarello and Claire Thompson for assistance with the manuscript, and Jack Muslovski for original photos and for many hours in the darkroom.

Sources for the photographs used throughout this work are indicated following each caption. The first and last photos are from the collection of the Stadium Corporation.

# PREFACE

When the Cleveland Landmarks Series was first conceived, the choice of topics for the first volume seemed rather obvious. Since the Terminal Tower is the city's most famous symbol, it appeared the logical choice to launch this series devoted to the landmarks of the Greater Cleveland area.

But when the time arrived to consider what the second topic should be, the choice seemed less clear. Since Cleveland is known as a city of culture, some thought was given to the museum complex in the University Circle area. The city is an industrial giant; consideration went towards describing the might of the Cuyahoga River valley. Greater Cleveland is renowned for its many fine residential areas; treatment of some of these was also pondered.

And then there was the Stadium on the lakefront. Cleveland Municipal Stadium had been the site of many thrills for uncounted area residents for a long time. Just how long a time? A little research turned up the fact that Cleveland Stadium would mark its fiftieth birthday in 1981. That decided the issue. Fifty years of service to the Greater Cleveland community seemed to call for some special recognition. And so it was that **Cleveland Municipal Stadium** became Volume 2 in the Cleveland Landmarks Series.

This Series originated out of a concern that too many Clevelanders failed to appreciate properly all of the fine things that mark the metropolitan area. It developed from the conviction that area residents too often magnified the region's problems while tending to overlook the achievements that have made, and continue to make, Cleveland a great city.

However much that may be true, another insight was gained after the publication of **The Terminal Tower Complex.** A tremendous number of people care, care deeply, about their city. They are anxious to talk about it and to read about it.

More important than that, however, is the expression of willingness to support those programs and undertakings which people believe will contribute to making Cleveland a better place to work and live.

Volume II is published with a deepened sense of hope and confidence in the city's future, and with gratitude to all those who have shown their support to the undertaking of this Series.

In many ways, the Stadium is analogous to the city. During events, it is "home" to many thousands. They ardently wish to see their side triumph. These hopes are sometimes rewarded; other times they are frustrated. But the people continue to return. Behind their support is a dream, a vision of victory, and the conviction that their loyalty will help make it come true.

The Stadium and the city have always found support in the people. It would seem that the people have backed real winners.

Seen from the vast expanse of the main parking lot (above), Cleveland Municipal Stadium offers a familiar and welcoming face to the arriving spectator. Seen from the gardens that border its northern perimeter (below), the Stadium seems a part of a rustic scene.     (Jack Muslovski)

# CHAPTER 1

## *The Lakefront*

In recent years, renewed interest has been shown in Cleveland's lakefront. A major expression of that interest was witnessed when the State of Ohio took responsibility for the improvement of the recreational lands along the Lake Erie shoreline. A multi-million dollar plan has been developed for the Cleveland State Lakefront Park.

The business community has also shown this interest. A campaign was undertaken to describe Cleveland in the national media as the "city on the north coast," pointing to its advantages as a port and transportation hub.

Interest in the lakefront, however, is not just a recent phenomenon. Cleveland's record of rapid growth from a small village into a major city was largely due to its location at the mouth of the Cuyahoga River where it meets Lake Erie. The pattern of the city's growth has been southward from the shoreline, and east and west from the banks of the river.

The properties developed nearest the lake and river are, of course, the oldest. As the years passed, they were the first to show signs of deterioration. By the time the twentieth century dawned, there was widespread recognition that something needed to be done to improve the lakefront area.

A plan for that purpose unfolded during the administration of Cleveland Mayor Tom L. Johnson (1901-1909). As the city and county expanded in population, there was a corresponding necessity for increases in city and county services. The need for development of a center for municipal and civic services became clear.

In 1902 a Group Plan Commission was established, led by architect Daniel H. Burnham. After a year of study the commission unveiled a plan for transforming the area bordering East Third Street, from Superior Avenue to the lakefront, into an impressive civic center.

The plan envisioned a swath of grass and trees running north along the East Third Street axis. Within this park-like setting would be erected a collection of governmental buildings, architecturally compatible, and stately in character.

This Group Plan (also known as the Mall Plan) took shape, beginning with the construction of the Federal Court House on Superior Avenue at Public Square. Then came the Cuyahoga County Court House and the Cleveland City Hall along Lakeside Avenue, on the bluff overlooking the lake. Later came the Public Auditorium and the Cleveland Board of Education buildings on the eastern perimeter of the development, and the Cleveland Public Library at its south end on Superior Avenue.

*Winter has removed the foliage from the Mall's many trees, but has provided a sprinkling of snow. Ringing the Mall, from left, are Public Auditorium, Cleveland Board of Education Building, Cleveland Public Library and the Federal Court House. East Third Street separates the Court building from the library.    (Jack Muslovski)*

To the north of the Court House and City Hall were the main railroad tracks running east and west. Together with lake, canal, and river shipping, these tracks had played a major role in the city's rapid growth toward its status as an industrial metropolis.

The location of the railroad tracks had prompted one additional feature in the Group Plan, a development that never materialized. Over and beyond the tracks a huge railroad passenger station had been planned. It was to be surrounded by gardens and plazas, right up to the shore line.

The station part of the Group Plan was not implemented because two brothers, Orris Paxton (O.P.) and Mantis James (M.J.) Van Sweringen, advocated another site for the passenger station, at the southwest quadrant of Cleveland's Public Square.

As is true of most plans in Cleveland, their proposal led to a protracted debate over the relative merits of the two sites. Ultimately the decision was made by the city's voters, when in 1919 they approved the Public Square location.

The result of that decision was the development of the Terminal Tower Complex on the Square and the termination of the Group Plan at the boundaries of Lakeside Avenue. While a vacuum was created in terms of specific plans to continue the governmental center, a recognition of the value of lakefront land was in no way diminished.

Between 1920 and 1930 some 300,000 carloads of fill material were dumped along the lakefront between West Third and East Ninth streets. The land was being prepared for some future development, even though it was not yet certain exactly what shape that might take.

*This view from the Justice Center shows the area which was once proposed as a platformed extension to the Mall. Just left of center the recently built Amtrak Station stands where the railroad station originally planned for the Mall was to have been constructed. (Jack Muslovski)*

*This airplane view of Cleveland's downtown lakefront, taken in the early 1920's, shows the site where the Stadium would eventually rise. Also missing from the skyline is the city's landmark, the Terminal Tower, also several years into the future. (The Cleveland Press)*

The first known suggestion that a stadium might occupy the land came from a supervisor of health and physical education for the Cleveland Board of Education. Floyd A. Rowe cited the need for a centrally located arena for high school athletic contests. He felt that the lakefront was admirably suited for such a purpose.

Nothing came of Rowe's idea until the administration of William R. Hopkins, Cleveland city manager. In 1921 Cleveland voters had approved a change in the city charter to provide city manager form of government. The new charter took effect in 1923, and Hopkins was named by city council to the new position.

Hopkins was a man of vision. It was his drive that led to the creation of Cleveland's main airport (today it bears his name) and for much of the development along the lakefront. The area to the east of East Ninth Street on which the downtown airport is situated was created as a result of Hopkins' lakefront development plans.

As Hopkins focused attention on the shoreline properties, renewed attention was given to the Group Plan, and how it could be carried out to the north of its existing boundaries. Many proposals were forthcoming.

*The lakefront is showing signs of landfill activity in this 1930 air view. The Stadium site, at the right, is ready for construction to begin; at the left, new land is being formed for the future Burke Lakefront Airport.* (Cleveland Public Library)

One idea was to build a terrace over the railroad tracks, extending the entire distance between West Third and East Ninth streets. Landscaped and tiered, the platform would provide a lakeshore garden entranceway to the cluster of municipal buildings in the Mall area.

A variant of this plan called for making the area a recreation center. This idea was popularly received, and with the recognition that the city lacked a facility for outdoors assembly of citizens, the stadium concept gained momentum. City Manager Hopkins appointed a new Group Plan Commission to make recommendations for a stadium use of the lakefront parcel. One recommendation was that a stadium should be built at the western end of the site, while at the eastern end an exhibition hall should be erected. A second proposal called for a large municipal swimming pool instead of the exhibit building.

The public's imagination was not intrigued by the hall or pool proposals, but the thought of a new municipal stadium excited civic leaders. A citizen's committee was formed, headed by long-time civic and business leader Charles A. Otis. Its purpose was to sell the project to the citizens; its membership comprised the business and political leadership of the city. One important name, however, was missing from the list.

Ernest S. Barnard had become president of the Cleveland Baseball Club in 1922 upon the death of its long-time owner, Jim Dunn. Barnard was deeply committed to the future of professional baseball in Cleveland and could clearly see the advantages which a large municipal stadium would offer to his Cleveland Indians team. At the same time, however, he was involved in trying to sell the baseball club which had been left to Jim Dunn's widow. He wanted to avoid appearing as though he were acting for a monetary benefit. Barnard had also been tapped to become the next president of the American League, and again felt that an active role in the Cleveland stadium campaign would be unseemly.

Nonetheless, Barnard worked quietly and devotedly behind the scenes, even to the point of assisting consultants on those aspects which would make the facility a perfect setting for professional baseball.

Baseball, however, was not the main thrust of the civic campaign. The committee detailed some 60 possible uses for a city-owned stadium, including pageants, dramatic offerings, musical entertainments, civic gatherings, business expositions, as well as athletic contests. In athletics alone, they claimed that the new facility could be used for boxing and wrestling matches, gymnastics, track and field events, skating, hockey, tennis, soccer, and even cricket, in addition to football and baseball. They foresaw the use of the stadium for all levels of sports, from the professional, through the college ranks, down to high school events.

The stadium campaign was directed at convincing voters to authorize a total of $2,500,000 in bond money for the construction project. An election for this purpose was set for November 6, 1928. The campaign's success in educating the public to the values of a new stadium was made clear that day, as voters responded 112,448 to 76,975 in favor of the project.

The unattractive landfill on the lakefront would soon disappear, to be replaced by a mammoth, shining, new, all-purpose recreational facility. The city waited for the first earth to be turned.

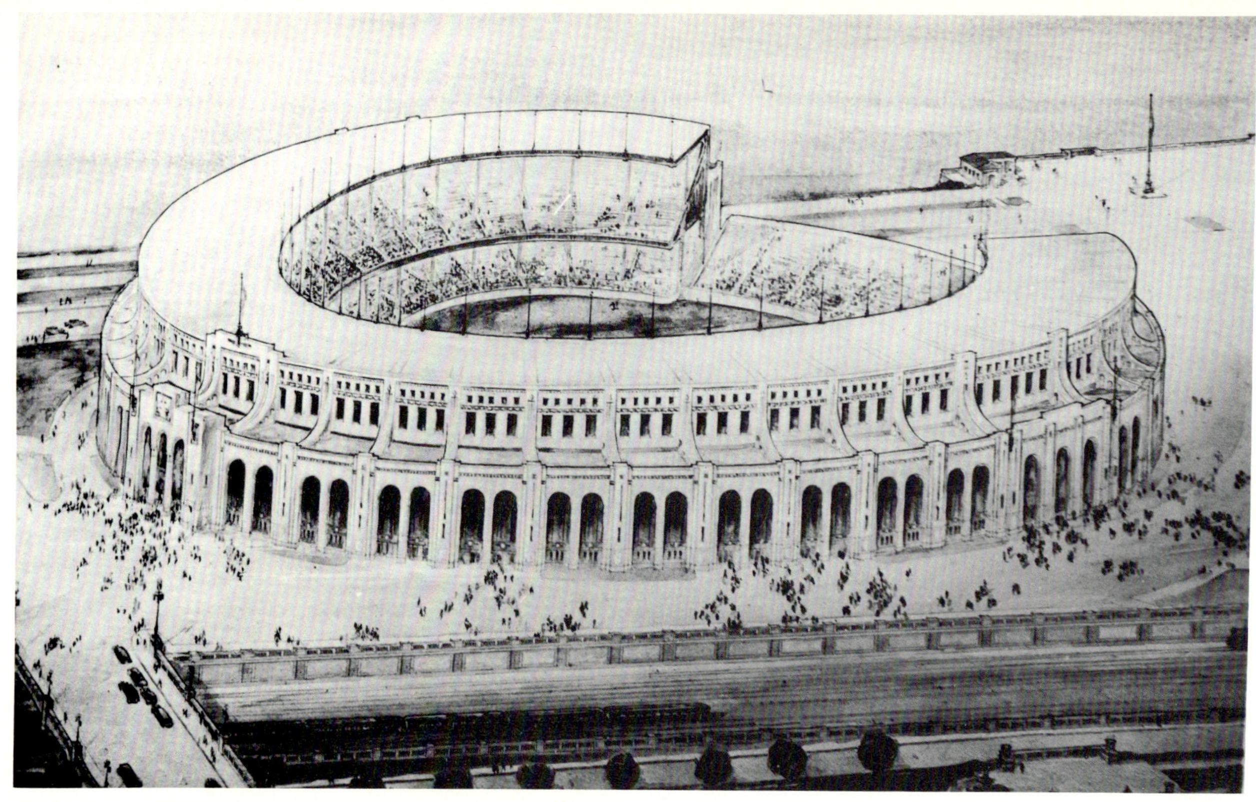

A picture is more effective than many words, and so those who were campaigning for the Stadium bond issue had this sketch prepared to show voters what the municipal facility would look like. Economics and other considerations brought about many subsequent changes in the design.    (Osborne Engineering Company)

With the election over, the construction site stood ready to be transformed by a swarm of building tradesmen. The site had been built up by landfill operations over the previous ten years.    (Osborne Engineering Company)

Anxious sidewalk superintendents did not expect construction of the Stadium to begin immediately upon passage of the bond issue, but they were hopeful that by the spring of 1929 they would see building activity on the site.

What had appeared to be the one obstacle to the plan, railroad rights to the Stadium site, had been worked out by City Manager Hopkins even before the election took place. The railroads had agreed to his proposal for a swap of land; they gave up their claims on the Stadium plot for a grant of city property to the west.

An obstacle to construction **did** appear in the form of a law suit by Andrew Meyer, a Cleveland voter. He contended in his action that the Stadium could not be built within the budget established by the bond issue, that the city had dubious legal title to the property, and that the enabling ordinance had been improperly worded. His suit was filed on May 29, 1929.

The suit did not interfere with planning for the Stadium. The mammoth project had been awarded to Walker and Weeks as consulting architects, and to the Osborne Engineering Company as project engineers.

Both firms came to the assignment with impressive credentials. Walker and Weeks already had to their credit in Cleveland several major buildings, including the Federal Reserve Bank Building on Superior Avenue, the Cleveland Public Library headquarters, and the National City Bank Building at East Sixth Street and Euclid Avenue. The firm was solidly established in the Cleveland architectural community.

The Osborne Engineering Company had been founded in Cleveland in 1892 by Frank C. Osborne. When selected for the Stadium project, it already had a national reputation in the field of stadium design. To its credit were such previous facilities as Yankee Stadium in New York City, Fenway Park in Boston, and Comiskey Park in Chicago. (Osborne Engineering is still headquartered in Cleveland and is still in the stadium design business. Recent examples of its work are RFK Stadium in Washington D.C. and Three Rivers Stadium in Pittsburgh).

In collaboration on an assignment such as Cleveland Municipal Stadium, the engineering firm was responsible for the basic design and structure — the functional aspects — while the architects worked with the plans to create an esthetically pleasing building.

Although the planning went forward, the threat to the project imposed by the lawsuit remained. It was some time before it disappeared. Meyer first took his case before district court, which decided in favor of the city. He then carried it to the Sixth District Court of Appeals in Cincinnati (where he lost once again), and finally appealed the case to the Ohio Supreme Court. On April 30, 1930, that court refused his request for an injunction against the Stadium project. The legal battle was over at last.

Yet one more obstacle arose to stand in the way of construction. William R. Hopkins, although he had done what most observers believed was a good job in moving the city forward, lost favor with the leadership of the political party which had given him the job. He was replaced as city manager by Daniel E. Morgan on January 27, 1930.

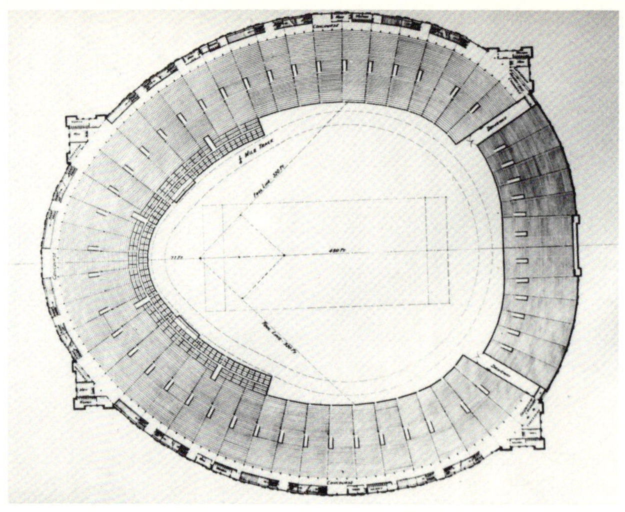

*While construction was delayed by a lawsuit, engineering and architectural work went ahead. In this drawing, the track, football and baseball fields are outlined against the seating plan for the main concourse and bleacher area. (Osborne Engineering Company)*

Morgan, like Hopkins, was a vigorous leader. As he examined the plans for the Stadium, he came up with some ideas which he thought would offer improvement. His concern was that the Stadium site was set too close to West Third Street, and that this would lead to traffic problems. He proposed that the Stadium be built at the geographic center of the Mall line as it crossed the lakeside property, approximately equidistant from West Third and East Ninth streets. Another controversy seemed in the making, but a compromise was reached. The Stadium location was moved one hundred feet to the east.

Still, before the first workman or the first piece of construction equipment could arrive at the Stadium site, bids had to be taken and contracts signed with various contractors and subcontractors. The successful bidder as general contractor for the project was the W. J. Schirmer Company of Cleveland. Major subcontractors included: Fifth City Excavating Company for grading work, Frederick Snare Corporation for the foundations, Bass Construction Company for steel work, Kahn Company for plumbing, and Parker Electric Company for wiring.

As the bids came in, it became clear that the original $2,500,000 budget for the Stadium was in jeopardy. Bulkheading and foundation work were proving to be more costly than had been anticipated. The task of providing the site with adequate roadways to handle patron traffic had also turned out to be more expensive than originally thought.

As a result, architects Walker and Weeks, and engineers Osborne Company were called in to see what recommendations they might make to reduce the costs of the building. The consultation brought about a few changes.

The Stadium had been conceived as a part of the Mall Plan, and so it had been originally designed with a stone facade which would keep its appearance in harmony with the other buildings in the group. Stone, however, was more costly than brick. As a cost-cutting step, the architects recommended that brick be used in place of stone for the exterior. Osborne Engineering decided that the bleacher section of the Stadium, because of its lighter weight load, could be erected without a pile foundation.

These and other minor adjustments brought the projected costs back to a closer correspondence with the voted budget.

The first contract to be let was for a bulkheading project. At last, on June 24, 1930, the first bulldozer arrived at the site. The sidewalk superintendents were finally going to have something to watch.

Reinforcing the site was deemed necessary for two reasons. First of all, since the Stadium area consisted largely of landfill material, bulkheading would provide for some real stability to the new land. Secondly, the north-south axis of the plot was too tight to provide for adequate parking along the northern side of the Stadium.

To solve these two problems, a new bulkhead was created in the lake. It pushed the land area two hundred feet further into Lake Erie, and an east-west stretch of nearly 1,300 feet was reinforced. Fill was dumped into the perimeters created by the new bulkhead until the newly-created land mass rose eight feet above the water line.

Grading the remainder of the site began almost immediately. The area extending from the West Third to the East Third street lines, and from the railroad tracks to the shoreline, had a large degree of variance to be made level. In some places it was only two feet above the surface of Lake Erie, while at others it stood as much as 40 feet above the water line. To grade the site as required for the project, a total of over 100,000 cubic yards of earth had to be excavated.

The foundation for the Stadium was the most demanding of the various construction tasks. Because of the nature of the land, the foundation cost nearly four times the amount that might have been expected had the Stadium been erected elsewhere.

*Piles for the Stadium's foundation were driven in clusters, then tied together with a concrete cap. The bottom part of the piles were wood, the top part made of a sleeve filled with concrete.* (Osborne Engineering Company)

*Progress was swift on the Stadium project. By January, 1931, the steel work was well advanced. In the foreground forms for the bleachers are nearing completion.     (Osborne Engineering Company)*

*Brick work has begun as the structural steel work is almost completed. Here Tower A is seen extending from the southwest corner of the building.     (Osborne Engineering Company)*

The foundation was by the pile method. Composite piles were used; the lower half was timber, and the upper part concrete. A total of 2,521 piles were used to provide a solid base for the building. Each pile was driven into the ground until the required resistance was met. In some cases, piles were hammered as deep as 65 feet. They were placed in clusters, and then tied together with a concrete cap, each cap serving as a base for structural steel work. Had all the piles been placed end to end, they could have formed a line extending nearly thirty-one miles.

The ribs of the Stadium began to take form as structural steel was put in place upon the foundation. The outer skin of the Stadium, brick and aluminum, came next, then the plumbing, electrical work, concrete, and roofing. The Stadium was beginning to take on its now-familiar appearance.

The workmen proceeded with their tasks at a rapid pace. An unusually mild winter further expedited their efforts. A total of four hundred workers could be found laboring on the project at any given time. Progress was swift, but it was marred by tragedy.

Weather on the sourthern edge of Lake Erie can be treacherous. On January 30, 1931, the winds off the lake were sharp and blustery. Their intensity that day snapped the cables holding a construction tower in place. As the scaffolding gave way, two steelworkers, Thomas Kelly and John Last, plunged 120 feet to their deaths.

Despite this tragedy and the occasional tricks of winter, the Stadium project moved ahead with speed. The huge building was completed on July 1, 1931, in an unbelievably brief span of just 370 days.

*Tragedy marred the construction story when this tower broke loose from the cable holding it as unusually gusty winds off the lake hit the project. Two workers who had been on top of the scaffolding were killed when the structure gave way. (Osborne Engineering Company)*

By March, 1931, (above) there still remained a great deal of work to do to complete the outer skin of the building. Just one month later (below) the Stadium stood virtually complete. Total construction time for the project was just 370 days. (Osborne Engineering Company)

And huge it was! To complete the facility, a phenomenal amount of building material was needed. Steel totalled 4,600 tons. Reinforced concrete ran to some 15,000 cubic yards. A million square feet of forms were used, and concrete flooring covered 123,000 square feet. A total of 3,300,000 bricks were laid in place, and 70 miles of electric wiring was snaked through 20 miles of conduit. Aluminum, weighing 130,000 pounds, was used for the upper walls, the largest construction use of that material to that time.

Cleveland Municipal Stadium was planned and built on the grand scale that characterized the thinking of the City of Cleveland during the first third of the twentieth century. Built with an eye to capturing the 1932 Olympic Games (which were subsequently awarded to Los Angeles), the Stadium was designed to meet a broad variety of uses and to be able to accommodate vast throngs of people.

The massive building measures 800 feet in length and 720 feet in width. A stroll around its outer walls would measure 2,640 feet, a half-mile excursion. It stands 115 feet tall, the equivalent of an 11-story building. The playing field measures three and one-half acres. The Stadium is so large that it would not quite fit in Cleveland's Public Square, occupying a total area of just under four and one-half acres of ground (the Square's dimensions are 660 by 622 feet).

The design of the Stadium aimed at minimizing its enormity. The architects placed two four-story towers at each end of the building, to create a sense of anchoring its oval shape to the site. To minimize the height, the upper portion of the structure has recessed walls sheeted with aluminum louvres. This recessed placement and change in exterior skin (from the brick below) takes away from the vertical thrust of the building.

*While the Stadium appears to be an oval, it is actually a polygon. Here can be seen the straight panels of brickwork, each slightly angled from the one adjoining it. The recessed upper portion of the building helped keep the Stadium from appearing clumsy in its size.* (Jack Muslovski)

The exterior is not truly oval, however. A close examination shows that the building's brick walls were laid in straight panels, slightly angled from the adjoining ones. This feature actually makes the Stadium into a polygon rather than an oval.

While esthetically treated to diminsh its ponderous dimensions, the building remains a giant. When compared with any other multi-purpose facility, it stands at the head of the list in size. Other stadiums have greater seating capacity for football, but they were not designed to be also compatible with baseball.

When built, the Stadium was the largest in the world to feature individual seats, rather than bleacher-type seating. Interestingly, the seats vary in size. Not only are the box seats closest to the field of action, they are also the widest, giving the patron a seating spread of twenty inches. The lower reserved seats (in front of the first set of columns) are nineteen inches wide; all the remaining seats in the house are eighteen inches. Seating was installed by the Theodor Kundtz Company.

The original seating capacity of the Stadium allowed for 37,896 seats in the main deck, 29,380 in the upper deck, and 10,913 in the bleachers. The seating capacity for the Stadium was thus established as 78,189. It was anticipated that additional seating could be added to the field area for football, thus increasing the seat count to about 90,000. For an event such as boxing, where almost the entire field area was available for patron seating, capacity could be further increased to a total of 110,000.

*The Stadium was the largest facility built to provide individual seating (rather than bleacher style) for its patrons. Most of the original seating remains, although the boxes have had the old wooden seats replaced by new plastic ones.   (Jack Muslovski)*

The playing field was installed by the firm of Henry J. Babcox and Son. The field area had to be plowed to a depth of eight inches, and all foreign material removed. Drainage tiles were then laid in place. Above the tiles, six inches of topsoil were added. To create the skin part of the infield for baseball, one part of clay was used for every two parts of sandy loam. Finally sod was placed, in a mixture of 60% Kentucky blue grass and 40% red top. Cinders were

with 1,000 watt lamps were installed around the inner ridge of the roof. Parker Electric Company did the installation.

The Stadium was designed with patron convenience in mind. A total of 48 turnstile entrances were built in the five main entrance gates, allowing for swift entry to the park. From the main concourse, 42 portals lead to the grandstand. Sixteen ramps were built up to the second level, and another eight lead to the upper deck. From there

*A total of 24 ramps were built to speed patrons to and from their seats. Throughout the planning stages, patron comfort and convenience were always given high priority.*                     (Jack Muslovski)

then spread around the outer perimeter of the field, an area designated for use as a track.

A late decision by the City was to add field lighting so that night events could take place. To accomplish this goal (for an additional $40,000) a string of 250 fixtures

another 38 portals lead to the seating area.

Lavatory facilities were located for maximum patron convenience, with 24 placed in service for each gender. A total of 25 drinking fountains were installed, and 38 concession stands were built.

When all was finally in readiness, with "Old Glory" flying from the flag poles, the community was invited down to the lakefront to see its newest facility. Free tours were given during the day on July 1, 1931, and formal opening festivities were planned to take place the following evening.

Before a crowd of better than 8,000, City Manager Daniel E. Morgan gave a welcoming address. He declared that the "ancient world never saw a structure like this."

Besides the speech making, the opening-nighters were treated to an evening of music, with many bands and a powerful chorus of 2,500 voices.

The years of campaigning, planning, litigation and construction were over. Cleveland's new Municipal Stadium was ushering in an era of community events that would keep the throngs coming year-in and year-out. Cleveland's lakefront had truly become a people-oriented place at long last.

*The newly completed Stadium stands reflecting the morning sun. The aluminum upper facing and the light brickwork below gave the new edifice a bright and sharp look.*          *(Osborne Engineering Company)*

# CHAPTER 3
## *Improvements*

Regardless of how well designed and how sturdily built a public facility may be, time inevitably calls for improvements to be made. Besides being kept structurally sound, a stadium must also satisfy the changing needs of its tenants and be inviting to patrons. Over the years a great many changes have been made, both to Cleveland Municipal Stadium and to its surroundings.

When they began their plans for the Stadium, the city fathers were aware that, as a public facility, it would not be a source of significant revenue for the city treasury. The purpose of a stadium or convention center, publicly owned, is to provide an attractive facility which will secure events of benefit to the community. To be able to do this effectively, rents and charges are kept low. The best that is hoped for is that income from these facilities will be sufficient to pay off capital indebtedness and provide funds for necessary upkeep. In other words, the goal is for a financial break-even operation.

Cleveland Municipal Stadium faced revenue problems right from the start. The city had counted heavily on signing a lease with the Cleveland Baseball Company. It would have made the Stadium the Cleveland Indians' home field and assured the city of a dependable income. As it was, however, the Indians did not make the Stadium their permanent home field until 1947 (more about the Indians in a later chapter).

In its first year of operation, 1931, the Stadium showed an operating loss of $1,778. That was the best figure the Stadium ever showed in terms of operating expenses. Even in 1948, a year in which the turnstiles clicked at a record pace, there was an overall loss of about $30,000.

In the years that the City of Cleveland itself was fiscally healthy, modest losses on the Stadium operation were not a serious problem. But as the city began to see its own financial condition worsening, finding the dollars to keep the Stadium a first-class facility became ever more of a chore.

Improvements to the Stadium can actually be divided into two categories: the first dealing with the area surrounding the facility and access to it, and the second, concerned with actual changes in the building itself. The early focus of the city was on the adjacent areas.

Although the Depression years had dimmed the prospects for further permanent additions to the Mall Plan, the city conceived a way to make the lakefront area next to the Stadium into a temporary entertainment center. The plan was to put on a major exposition, modeled after the Century of Progress festival which had been held in Chicago in 1933.

The area which now serves as the main parking lot for the Stadium (from the Stadium east to East Ninth Street) was selected as the site for the Great Lakes Exposition. Joined to the Mall above by a bridge, the entire exposition spread from the Public Auditorium, out across the Mall, and down to the lake's edge. The exposition opened on June 28, 1936, and served as the official celebration of the centennial of Cleveland's incorporation as a city. Over the exposition's acreage, dozens of buildings were erected, shrubbery planted, and marvelous lighting displays installed. The Exposition had for its theme the kind of industrial and technological expertise that could be found in the Greater Cleveland area.

*In 1936 and 1937 the Cleveland lakefront was transformed by the Great Lakes Exposition. In its two-year run, it attracted over 7,000,000 to the celebration in honor of the city's centennial.*            *(Cleveland Public Library)*

As far as the city was concerned, the Exposition was a great success on two counts. It provided for a splendid vehicle to celebrate the city's anniversary, and it dressed up the lakefront at little cost to the city's coffers. Local business and industry had rallied to the call and provided for almost all of the exhibition's cost.

One of the most beautiful achievements of the show was the building of gardens immediately north of the Stadium. Under the sponsorship of the Garden Club of Cleveland, they were planned by Donald Gray, the garden editor of the Cleveland **Press.** Sporting thousands of annuals, varieties of trees, shrubs, rose bushes, an electric fountain, and terraced walkways, the garden was one of the most popular attractions for Great Lakes Exposition visitors.

*One of the most popular attractions at the Exposition was the Donald Gray Gardens, located immediately north of the Stadium.*     *(Cleveland Public Library)*

*Work on extending Erieside Drive, to connect the Stadium's eastern and western access roads, was begun in the mid-1940s. This and other landfill projects over the years have gradually moved Lake Erie's waters farther from the Stadium. (The Cleveland Press)*

More than 7,000,000 people from all parts of the country visited the fair during its two-year run. When it closed, after the 1937 season, its temporary buildings were removed. The gardens, however, remained and stand to this day as the sole witness to those days of celebration.

Unfortunately, time has not treated the gardens kindly. Built north of the Stadium, they abutted the waters of the lake. As the years passed, erosion began to threaten them. In 1946, the city announced a plan that would both save the gardens and provide for better traffic flow for Stadium crowds. Additional fill was to be brought to the lakefront and deposited to the north of the gardens. On this newly created land, Erieside Avenue would be extended from East Ninth Street, beyond the parking lots where it then terminated, to circle north of the gardens and connect with West Third Street.

While that plan did save the gardens from slowly crumbling into Lake Erie, a general failure to maintain their landscaping has allowed the once-beautiful setting to deteriorate into an overgrown and weed-infested shadow of its former beauty. From the Stadium today, many observers wonder about the pillars that line the north roadway. Few realize these ''ruins'' are the legacy of a city in celebration.

*Access to the Stadium was made much easier by the construction of the freeway along the lakefront. Here a final connecting link is being placed into the Main Avenue Bridge which joined east and west segments of the shoreway in 1939. (Cleveland Public Library)*

Following the exhibition, the next major change in the Stadium's surroundings occurred in 1938. In that year construction began on the 8,000 foot Main Avenue Bridge that would link the eastern and western portions of the then-abuilding Lakeshore Freeway. As the graceful bridge structure neared the Stadium, it necessitated the removal of a pedestrian passage connecting the facility with the terrace behind the County Court House. So while the new freeway made automobile access to the Stadium much easier, it diminished the convenience for those approaching the park by foot.

Just as the Main Avenue Bridge suggested the growing importance of the automobile, so too, at the opposite end of the Stadium property, another manifestation took place. For years, patrons of the lakefront and the East Ninth Street Pier could catch a streetcar along upper East Ninth Street and be transported to the foot of the roadway, where it met Erieside Avenue. There the streetcar would enter a loop in what is today the extreme northeast end of the main Stadium parking lot. But as people abandoned public transit for their private cars, and as the need for parking space correspondingly increased, the streetcar line came to seem more an obstacle than a convenience. On October 3, 1938, the Cleveland Railway Company ended service on the line, and the tracks were removed.

One expenditure for the Stadium itself was undertaken in these early years, although it was not a planned one. On October 13, 1936, an explosion rocked the lakefront facility, shattering windows, cracking grandstand concrete in three sections, and ripping out some 500 seats. Inspectors rushed to the scene, fearing at first that a bomb had gone off. Investigation revealed that the cause of the explosion had actually been frayed electrical wiring sparking gas from a leaking line. Fortunately, no one was in the vicinity at the time, and there were no injuries. The city spent $18,000 for repairs and made sure that there could be no future repetition of the incident.

One of the major changes that the Stadium required centered on its capacity for lighting the field for evening athletic contests. In 1931, night-time sports were not a very common practice. As time went on, however, their popularity greatly increased. With this change, it became clear that original lighting was not really satisfactory.

*The Stadium showed the effects of an explosion which was blamed on a leaking gas line and faulty wiring. The freak 1936 accident cost the city $18,000 in repair bills.    (The Cleveland Press)*

The 250 original 1,000 watt lamps gave way to 716 bulbs in 1945, to 796 in 1948, and to 1,318 by 1950. That number remains the same today.

As the Stadium eventually became more frequently used (in 1947 both the Indians and the Browns called it home), attention focused on other requirements for making the Stadium more suitable to modern demands.

In 1949 a new ramp from the Mall to the Stadium was built. This structure was meant to make up for the pedestrian bridge that had been lost to freeway construction some nine years earlier.

*Access to the Stadium has always been a major concern of management. In 1949 a new pedestrian bridge over the railroad tracks provided an easy route to the Stadium from the Mall.    (The Cleveland Press)*

In 1950, a new ticket office was built at Gate A for the Cleveland Indians, and auxiliary scoreboards were installed on the facing of the upper deck. These improvements, together with the new lighting, cost the city about $350,000.

In 1953, the main Stadium scoreboard was improved with new wiring and lighting. In 1961 the board was further redesigned to provide for trumpet fanfares, flaring gas jets, fireworks, and fan messages. A new exterior was put on the old frame, giving the scoreboard a more contemporary look.

The city was not only interested in keeping the tenants and patrons happy; it also was concerned that the representatives of the media which covered Stadium events should have reasonably comfortable surroundings.

A major need was for a football pressbox. In 1960, a new facility was built at the top of the upper deck in sections 7-9. While this provided for a good view of the action on the field, it did require a rather arduous climb. Additional boxes were built on the roof for use by coaches and broadcasters, and for filming game action. Access to the rooftop boxes was provided through the football pressbox.

Two years later, the writers and broadcasters were further treated when the Wigwam, the pressroom in Tower A, was completely refurbished. The Wigwam serves as a center for press conferences and also as a dining room for accredited journalists.

Those covering baseball did not have to wait long for a new facility of their own. In 1965 a new baseball pressbox costing $200,000 was constructed, stretching from sections 19 through 25; it could accommodate 110 writers.

*The football pressbox, installed in 1960, offers the reporting entourage a good view of the action. Its location, at the top of the upper grandstand, required the scribes to make a considerable climb. That problem was eliminated in 1981 when an elevator was installed.* (Jack Muslovski)

Construction to create a ring of 108 loges was the first major undertaking of the newly formed Stadium Corporation. Here work is underway in early 1974 on the first of the bilevel luxury units. *(Stadium Corporation)*

Each Stadium loge is fully furnished, has storage and lavatory facilities, is equipped with closed-circuit television, and is air-conditioned. Annual rental fees, which climbed to $24,500 in 1981, have not diminished the loges' popularity with Cleveland's corporate community. *(Jack Muslovski)*

The loges, which are suspended from the bottom of the upper deck, provide for a good view of the field action. Each unit provides outdoor as well as indoor seating. *(Jack Muslovski)*

These loges, completed in April, 1975, proved to be immensely popular with the Cleveland business community. Available on a yearly rental basis, the initial rental figure for the loges was $15,000 for an eight-seat loge (of which there are 84) and $10,500 for a six-seat loge (of which there are 24). The rental figure includes season tickets for all home baseball and football games, parking, and cleaning and maintenance service.

The loges are heated for winter comfort and air-conditioned to moderate summer temperatures. Each is equipped with indoor and outdoor seating. Other furnishings include: refrigerator, sink, coffee maker, and television. The television is wired to receive regular broadcasting as well as Stadium closed circuit pictures. Each loge also has a storage closet and lavatory.

The annual rental fee for the loges has risen each year (costs in 1981 are $24,500 and $17,500 respectively), but their popularity with the community remains unabated, and there is a sizeable waiting list of interested potential clients.

While the loges represented the most spectacular of the improvements undertaken by the Stadium Corporation, they were by no means the only one. Another major undertaking involved the building of a new scoreboard.

Scoreboard technology had continued to become more sophisticated, so that the 1961 improvements to the original board were no longer adequate for modern needs. A new scoreboard was begun in February, 1977, with a price tag of $1,500,000. Containing 21,000 lights, the board is controlled through a computer located in the baseball pressbox. There, three computer terminals control the messages that appear across the huge scoreboard screen, the largest single matrix scoreboard installation to that time. The three terminals replaced the original operating controls which had consisted of 5,580 buttons. The new board took more than a year to complete; it premiered with the opening of the 1978 baseball season.

Still another major project involved the replacement of 11,000 old wooden seats with new molded plastic ones. This improvement, like the others, was made for the sake of increasing patron comfort and enjoyment.

The field also received attention. At the end of the 1975 football season the field was completely dug up and new drainage tiles laid into place. The field was lowered in order to improve patron viewing from the lower box seats. A new surface of natural grass (Merien Blue) was laid in. Natural turf was preferred over artificial by members of the teams using the field, who felt it would provide them with a safer playing environment.

*The scoreboard computer room provides an excellent view of the field. Here three computer terminals are used to transmit messages to the new scoreboard which was put into action in 1978.* (Stadium Corporation)

*The Stadium's well-conditioned field became a sea of mud in 1975 as the entire surface was dug up to provide for better drainage. The field's level was also lowered to allow better viewing from the box seats.* (Stadium Corporation)

The choice of natural surface probably pleased most members of the community as well, for Cleveland has had the good fortune of being served by a groundskeeping dynasty which for many years has enjoyed the respect and appreciation of the fans and the teams alike. It was in 1935 that Cleveland Indians' president Alva Bradley brought Emil Bossard to take care of the fields at old League Park and at the Stadium. He was joined by sons Harold, Marshall, and Gene (who later left to serve the White Sox at Chicago's Comiskey Park).

The care which the Bossard family lavished on the field over the years earned them a national reputation. Their wizardry at tailoring the field so as to take advantage of the home team's strengths, made them not so much groundskeepers but almost members of the teams.

The Bossard family continues to work for the Stadium Corporation, with the third generation, grandson Brian, having taken charge in 1979. Of the 15-25 men needed for field services, seven are members of the Bossard family (among whom the fourth generation is now represented).

Other important, if less obvious, renovation was also undertaken by the Stadium Corporation. Over $2,000,000 was expended for better plumbing and wiring. Major improvements were made to the lavatories, to the concession stands, and in general brightening and repair work. In 1981, a new elevator was installed to provide better access for handicapped patrons (and also to ease the climb of football writers to their lofty pressbox).

While improvements were going on inside the Stadium others were being made outside. In 1973 the City of Cleveland and Cuyahoga County began construction of major new garages behind City Hall and the County Court House. The Willard Park and Huntington Park garages added more than 2,200 convenient parking slots for Stadium patrons.

During work on the garages the ramp connecting the Mall with the Stadium had to be disconnected, temporarily inconveniencing patrons who were left with only two approaches from the downtown area. The ramp was reconnected in August, 1977.

As the Stadium marks its fiftieth birthday in 1981, the Stadium Corporation has spent $8,200,000 for renovations since it took charge in 1974. During the years since it was first built, five times the Stadium's original cost has been expended to keep it a first-class facility.

The improvements have had their effect. A renewed interest in the Stadium has been shown in all parts of the Greater Cleveland area. As the park has been improved, security augmented, comfort enhanced, and access eased, a new pride in the facility has been kindled.

As a patron moves up the ramps from the concourse to the grandstand and looks about at the venerable giant in its new attire, that same sense of awe and excitement is generated as when the Stadium first opened. Cleveland Municipal Stadium remains very close to the hearts of the people of Northern Ohio.

*Other improvements undertaken by the Stadium Corporation included refurbishing the Stadium Restaurant (above), which is open daily for lunch and on evenings when games are scheduled, and rebuilding concession stands (below) along the Stadium concourses. The new concession stands provide for faster and more orderly food service.* (Jack Muslovski)

# CHAPTER 4

## *Events*

Cleveland Municipal Stadium can certainly lay claim to being one of the nation's great arenas in terms of size and versatility. But what makes the Stadium a special kind of place is only marginally related to its dimensions and architecture. Bricks and concrete, steel and aluminum alone cannot capture the essence of such a place.

One must leave the tangible behind and take a journey into history. Cleveland's collective memory about its venerable Stadium is a rich one. It is the repository of countless thrills and excitement, of moments of awe and reverence.

That memory is made up of more events than can be retold. It is filled with exciting contests, thrilling stunts, religious and civic celebrations, musical and artistic presentations, and intense rivalries. Behind each memory is the roar of the crowd, for the Stadium can really be understood only as a place for people.

Probably for most Greater Clevelanders, the first thought of the Stadium centers on its being the home of the Cleveland Indians baseball team and the Cleveland Browns football squad. Their role in the Stadium's history is truly a significant one (the next two chapters are devoted to them), but just as the Stadium was not conceived as being exclusively a center for sports, so too its history has been filled with just about every kind of event.

In some ways the Stadium stands as a symbol for the genuinely universal interests of the Greater Cleveland community. It is not just in sports that Cleveland has been a major draw; the city also stands as a central stop for many kinds of entertainment. Cleveland has been, and continues to be, "big league" in its support of a variety of people-oriented events, and the Stadium has been the locale for a great percentage of them.

The first major event to be held at the Stadium took place on July 3, 1931, a boxing match for the heavyweight championship of the world. Fight promoters, hoping the excitement that the new stadium would generate might swell the crowd, worked hard to build up enthusiasm for the fight.

Max Schmeling had won the heavyweight title in a bout with Jack Sharkey in New York City the previous year. This match between him and Young Stribling was Schmeling's first defense of his title. As such, it lacked some of the excitement that had existed in the series of earlier Jack Dempsey fights. Thus, while the promoters thought about Cleveland's 110,000 boxing seat capacity, the crowd for the event never approached that figure. However, a good crowd of 37,396 did show up to witness Schmeling win by TKO in fifteen rounds.

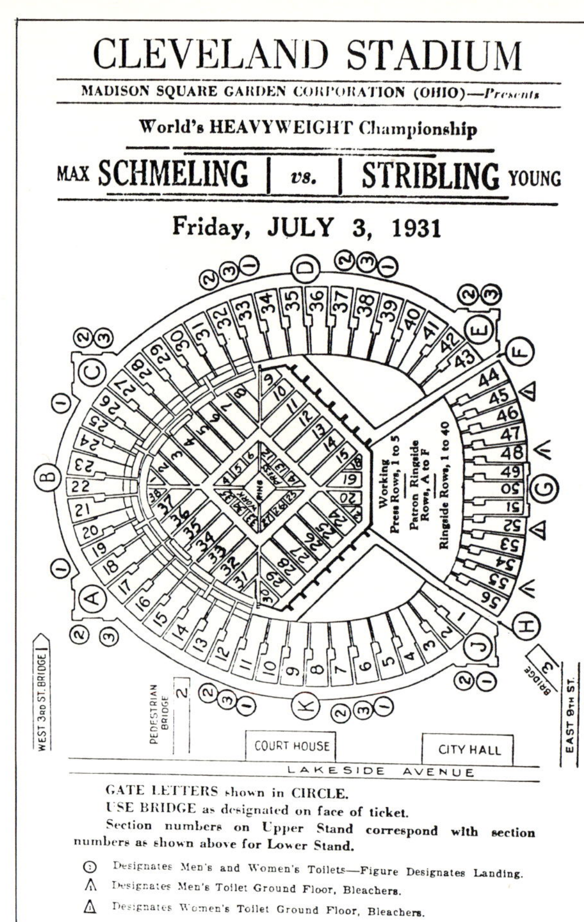


This was the program that greeted patrons to the first event held at Cleveland Municipal Stadium, a fight for the heavyweight championship between Max Schmeling and Young Stribling, July 3, 1931. *(Osborne Engineering Company)*

The setup for the opening event shows the field turned over to patron seating. By using the field to the maximum for this purpose, seating capacity for an event such as boxing could be increased to 110,000. *(Osborne Engineering Company)*

Two weeks later, the Stadium saw its first baseball game. During the week of July 14, 1931, the Shrine held its national convention in Cleveland. With all the color that marks such a spectacle, conventioneers headed to the Stadium for a parade and ball game. Koran Shrine played Al Sirat Grotto before a crowd of 26,000 and won 6-1

The focus then turned away from sports and to — of all things — grand opera. Cleveland had established itself as a significant supporter of opera, and had been represented on the annual tour of the Metropolitan Opera Company since 1924 (at the present writing, Cleveland holds the record as the best attended tour event for the national company). So it seemed a natural outgrowth of Cleveland's interest in grand opera to give the city opera in a truly grand setting, such as the new Stadium offered.

Sponsored by The Cleveland **Press,** opera week was held in the Stadium beginning on July 28. An operatic performing stage, 300 feet by 125 feet, was built across the infield area. The house was limited to seating in the western portion of the grandstand, in the areas nearest home plate. Tickets for the operas cost from 25 cents to two dollars.

With a cast made up of stars from the Metropolitan and Chicago opera companies a variety of operatic works were produced, including **Aida, Cavalleria Rusticana, Carmen, La Gioconda, Die Meistersinger,** and **The Bartered Bride.** Whatever tributes might legitimately be paid to the Stadium, fine acoustic properties, so essential to opera, cannot be included in the list. While the setting and stagecraft were impressive, music lovers were disappointed in the quality of the sound. That week was the only time opera was performed at the Stadium.

*Opera Week at the Stadium featured the largest stage ever constructed for an operatic performance. Seating was limited to the sections located between the two baseball dugouts.*  (The Cleveland Press)

On September 6, 1931, the first crowd to truly test the Stadium's capacity arrived — for a religious event. The Roman Catholic Diocese of Cleveland's Holy Name Society rented the facility for a prayer service in honor of then-Bishop Joseph Schrembs' tenth annivesary as the head of the diocese. A throng of about 70,000 gathered on a Sunday afternoon to pay tribute to their bishop. For the first time the sounds of the crowd were directed towards realities above, rather than to the field below.

The very next day, Labor Day, the Cleveland Federation of Labor was responsible for having the first soccer match played in the Stadium. Another sport had made its lakefront debut.

Football debuted on the evening of September 9, 1931. The Cleveland Indians (an early Cleveland entry into the still strug-gling National Football League) played an exhibition game with the semi-pro Pennzoil team. A crowd of 35,000 made its way to the lakefront park to see the home team defeat its opponent by a score of 10-0.

College football was next to appear. The honor of the premiere college event goes to Cleveland's Jesuit university, John Carroll. Carroll opted to use the Stadium as its home field for the entire 1931 schedule. The first game, against Adrian College, took place on September 24; it brought Carroll a 26-6 victory before a crowd numbering just over 2,000.

John Carroll continued to make the Stadium its home field through 1935, and played there regularly through the early 1950's. The local school has the distinction of having played more football games at the Stadium than any other college.

*John Carroll University called the Stadium its home field for football for several years. Here the Blue Streak Squad of 1932 poses for a team picture at its practice site.* (*John Carroll University*)

High school football's Stadium inaugural also occurred in 1931. A crowd of about 8,500 paid their way to see two Cleveland high schools, East Tech and West Tech, battle to a scoreless tie on the evening of October 3. It was the first time that a Cleveland Scholastic Senate game had ever been played under lights.

In 1931 the Stadium was selected as the site of the annual championship high school game, pitting the winners of the city's East and West Senate titles in a contest for the city crown.

The first game was played between Cathedral Latin School and Central High School, with Latin winning 18-0. The championship series was a popular one and continued at the Stadium until 1970. Eleven times the games drew crowds of more than 40,000; five games drew over 50,000 fans. The largest crowd for the high school championship game was in 1946, when 70,955 saw Cathedral Latin blast Holy Name 35-6. Benedictine High School holds the record for the most appearances in the Stadium classic with 16.

Interest in the game, played around the Thanksgiving holiday, began to fade in the middle 50's, but then picked up momentum in the early 60's. In 1968 heavy rains held the crowd to just 17,582. Planners thought that a change in format might help, so in 1969 a doubleheader was scheduled. Benedictine defeated St. Ignatius 18-7, and St. Joseph defeated St. Edward 22-0, but attendance dipped another 2,000. The doubleheader format was tried once more in 1970, but at that game only 10,994 were in attendance.

With competition from professional football on television, the complications of family holiday plans, and the cold weather of November on Cleveland's lakefront, the series' attractiveness had waned. Championship games continued after 1970, but from then on they were held at smaller fields.

*Cathedral Latin is about to score again in its 35-6 win over Holy Name High School in the 1946 city championship high school football game at the Stadium. The crowd of 70,955 that year set the record for the popular annual schoolboy classic.    (The Plain Dealer)*

*Seats were modestly priced for the first in the series of Navy-Notre Dame football games played at the Stadium. An end-zone seat cost $2.20 for the inaugural game.   (Osborne Engineering Company)*

Another popular series held at the Stadium over the years was a college rivalry between Notre Dame and Navy football squads. The first in the series was held in 1932, with Notre Dame defeating Navy 12-0 before 61,554 fans. In the next contest in 1934, Navy took a measure of revenge by defeating Notre Dame 10-6 in front of a crowd of 57,124. These two teams played again in 1939, 1942, 1943, 1945, 1947, 1950, 1952, and after a lapse of several years, again in 1976 and 1978. Over this stretch of 11 games, Navy managed but one victory and one tie (1945). The series drew 767,036 fans to the Stadium. The best crowd, 84,090, attended in 1947, witnessing a 27-0 rout by Notre Dame. Average attendance for the series is 69,730.

There have been many other football games in the Stadium over the years. Cleveland's old Western Reserve College and Case Institute of Technology have both hosted games there, as has Ohio State University. Ohio State played Illinois there in 1942 and Purdue in 1943. Great Lakes Academy played against Pitt in 1942, and the Cleveland Rams of the National Football League played an exhibition game against the Midwest College All-Stars in 1941.

As much as the Stadium is associated with sports, however, the all-time attendance record for an event there was set by a religious celebration! In 1935 Cleveland was selected as the site for the Seventh Eucharistic Congress of the Roman Catholic Church. The Congress' purpose was to foster devotion to the church's beliefs about the presence of Jesus Christ within the Eucharistic sacrament.

Catholicism has always been able to provide marvelous pageants. Its liturgy, vestments, and its colorful rituals, together with a tremendous response from its adherents, made Cleveland the center of a very colorful and moving convention.

Because of the tremendous crowds that attended the public events of the Congress, it became necessary to use the Stadium in addition to the indoor facilities of the city's convention center.

On Saturday, September 24, 1935, 75,000 men attended a midnight Mass in the Stadium. At the consecration of the liturgy, the Stadium lights were extinguished, and the only illumination in the shadowy park came from 75,000 lighted tapers. It was an eerie but awe-inspiring sight to see the gigantic Stadium and the huge crowd by candlelight.

*The Stadium was an eerie sight at midnight, September 24, 1935 as 75,000 Catholic men held lighted tapers during a Mass celebrated as part of the program of the Seventh Eucharistic Congress.*                    *(Catholic Universe Bulletin)*

*The all-time largest crowd in Stadium history gathered for the closing service of the Eucharistic Congress. Here part of the throng of 125,000 is seen forming a "living monstrance" across the playing field area.*                    *(Catholic Universe Bulletin)*

The next day, the finale of the Congress, a crowd of more than 300,000 flooded into downtown Cleveland to see a procession in which the Eucharist was carried from St. John the Evangelist Cathedral, at East Ninth Street and Superior Avenue, to the Stadium. The procession consisted of parochial school children in their uniforms, various lay groups in organizational dress, the religious and priests of the Diocese in clerical garb, and most of the bishops of the country, in full episcopal regalia. Last in the colorful procession came Patrick Cardinal Hayes of New York City, carrying the Eucharistic monstrance (a vessel which holds a large host for viewing by the people).

It took three hours for the procession to wend its way to the Stadium. There, every seat was filled. Thousands stood at the rear of the grandstands. The field had been outlined by 100,000 flowers in the shape of a monstrance. Into that floral outline came the 22,000 marchers. Altogether a crowd of 125,000 jammed into the Stadium that afternoon for the Benediction service. The Stadium's all-time record crowd was one that came out to "cheer" for the Lord.

One of the most interesting events of 1939 was a double bill. The audience was treated to the music of Benny Goodman and his band as well as the action of a Wild West Rodeo.

To get ready for the event, the Stadium field was filled with all the equipment necessary for typical rodeo stunts. There were ramps for motorcycle competitions, a brick wall through which a car would hurtle, flaming board walls along the track for cars to race through, and, of course, corrals for the animals. There were bronco riding, calf roping, and exhibitions of all kinds of riding skills.

Benny Goodman played for a jitterbug jamboree and then, later in the program, put on one of his famous swing concerts. A crowd of 44,267 was delighted by the festivities.

*Patriotic and civic celebrations were a prominent part of the Stadium's schedule through most of its history. Here a 1940 crowd salutes the American flag.    (The Plain Dealer)*

*Fireworks have been a perennial favorite with Stadium crowds. They have been used with football games, baseball contests, and with various civic events. Not only do they cause the Stadium to rock with sound, but they offer those anywhere near the facility a spectacular aerial display.      (Stadium Corporation)*

As events in Europe and the Far East moved nearer to the eruption of World War II, there developed all across the country an increased sense of patriotism and appreciation for the blessings of liberty. In Cleveland, this sensitivity was translated into the first Festival of Freedom, which was held at the Stadium on July 4, 1939.

In its inaugural, the festival featured an orchestra, a community sing-along, a parade of flags, a nationality pageant, speeches, and a fireworks show. The following year a crowd of 75,000 gathered in a darkened Stadium. Each person there struck a light for liberty, holding high a flaming match.

The Festival of Freedom grew in popularity with each year. The Stadium would be filled with 80,000-plus crowds, with thousands more gathered outside to watch the fireworks display. It was the growing crowds and the fact that fireworks were the highlight of the event that led to the festival being moved from the Stadium in 1950. In that year it took place at Lakefront Airport where a crowd of nearly 200,000 watched the aerial spectacular. Not only did the airport setting provide more room for the spectators, it also allowed a better arrangement for positioning the fireworks.

In 1954 the festival was moved westward along the Shoreway to Edgewater Park. The reason for the move was that the Cleveland Indians were scheduled to play a night game (the Tribe was in an exciting pennant race and a large crowd was expected for the game) at the Stadium on the same night the festival had been planned. Authorities were sure that downtown Cleveland could not accommodate the crowd that the two events would generate. The festival has been held at Edgewater Park ever since.

As the war years moved on, more interest centered on the military and in supporting the war effort against the Axis. In 1942 The Cleveland **News** sponsored a boxing card at the Stadium, with the proceeds being earmarked for "Bombers for MacArthur" (the general was at that time preparing his next step towards the Philippines as he mopped up Japanese resistance in New Guinea). A crowd of 23,574 turned out for the boxing matches and to show their support for the war effort.

It was just a short while later, on September 14, 1942, that it looked as though Cleveland's lakefront had been invaded. Over 2,000 troups arrived in 400 railroad cars to set up a bivouac area just east of East Ninth Street at the lakefront. It was the Army Show, whose purpose was to educate the population on the war cause and to earn proceeds for the Army Emergency Relief Fund.

All week after their arrival, the army men worked at setting up the parking areas around the Stadium as a model "Battle Depot," an exhibit of military machinery, guns, tanks, and even captured German and Japanese planes.

The city's three daily newspapers gave the Army Show good publicity, building up enthusiasm for a series of mock battles that would take place nightly at the Stadium, beginning September 18.

A crowd of 36,732 came to the first performance, on a Friday night. No sooner had they taken their seats, than there was a roar above as warplanes buzzed the Stadium. No one was seated in the bleacher section, because it had been converted into a model fortified Japanese village.

The war game simulation lasted just over an hour and a half. In that time howitzers, mortars, machine guns, and aerial cannon fired volley after volley at the "enemy position." The din was overwhelming, putting to shame by comparison the thunder of the always popular fireworks displays. And best of all, the home troops were victorious in the battle.

So impressed were the first night patrons that the crowd the next day jumped to 54,432, then to 63,201, and on Monday night to 76,654, with the final night drawing 60,601. In five days the Army Show drew 291,620, all of whom by their presence made a contribution to the Relief Fund. Ticket prices for the show ranged from 55 cents to $2.20.

*The Jehovah's Witnesses have assembled at the Stadium on more than one occasion for their district meeting. Here a capacity crowd awaits the start of a convention service.* (The Cleveland Press)

In 1946 another major religious event was scheduled for the Stadium. The Jehovah Witnesses held their district meeting in Cleveland, with the Stadium being the site for the chief gatherings. A crowd of 80,000 thronged the Stadium for the assembly. The general citizenry, still highly sensitive to any potential lack of patriotism, raised a cry that the United States flag was not flying above the Stadium. The protesters thought this was due to the Witnesses' belief that a flag was a form of graven image, and as such, prohibited by Biblical injunction. The city investigated the complaints and found that the flag's absence was due to oversight of the Stadium staff rather than to any concern attributable to the Witnesses. The fury quickly subsided. The assembly continued; converts made during the convention were taken from the park out to Edgewater Beach for baptism in the waters of Lake Erie.

The Jehovah Witnesses returned to the Stadium in 1975 for their district assembly, attracting over 213,000 interested parties to the four days of their June meeting.

The summer of 1947 was a busy one for the Stadium, but one which also included a great deal of controversy. In growing popularity at the time was the sport of midget auto racing. Sponsored by Cleveland Raceways, Inc., the sport was booked into the Stadium on a trial basis.

To make the field suitable for the midget races, a good deal of work had to be done. Ten feet of sod on the inner side of the track area had to be removed in order to provide a 30-foot wide racing strip. A rail 18-inches high had to be built along the inner track line. The track itself had to be torn up and its cinders replaced with clay. These modifications cost the Raceway sponsor over $25,000.

A controversy erupted, centering on the complaints of the Cleveland Indians and groundskeeper Emil Bossard. Both felt that baseball and auto racing were not compatible, that the modifications to the track were likely to lead to injuries for the ballplayers. Despite the protests, Cleveland Mayor Thomas A. Burke signed the lease permitting the midget cars to appear.

The first race was held June 14, 1947 and such leading figures from the auto world as Mauri Rose, Al Bonnell and Bill Holland competed. A crowd of 21,197 came to the inaugural event; many were splashed with mud as the midget autos rapidly converted the newly-laid track into a washboard.

A second race took place the following weekend, with 16,565 fans in attendance. During the event an accident occurred in which driver Bill Boyd was injured when his car rolled over.

The third race was held on August 2 and left the field in such a disastrous condition that Mayor Burke exercised his prerogative under the terms of the lease, and vetoed any further use of the Stadium for auto racing.

The confrontation over the midget racers led to a revision in the lease which the baseball club had with the city. Thereafter a clause was written into their agreement that would govern other uses to which the Stadium might be put. Language in contracts with other groups provided that their use of the Stadium was permitted only "upon condition that there be obtained the consent of the Cleveland Baseball Co."

The 1947 calendar for the Stadium gives a good indication of the kinds of events that the facility would host in the years to follow.

*Midget Auto racing was tried at the Stadium in 1947. During the second event in the controversial series, driver Bill Boyd sustained serious injuries when his racing car overturned.    (The Cleveland Press)*

In that year it was the home field for 77 Cleveland Indians' games and for seven Browns' football games. Besides the three racing events, also scheduled were the Festival of Freedom, a midget airplaine rac ing contest, an outdoors sports show, a Veterans of Foreign Wars' convention, and the annual Baseball Federation Amateur Day (that year's program was the 38th in a series that helped raise funds for the city's amateur hardball program). In addition to these, Cathedral Latin School played two games at the Stadium, as did John Carroll University. There was a Notre Dame-Navy football tilt and the annual championship high school football charity classic. The 1947 year was the busiest the Stadium had to that time.

In 1949 the Cleveland Athletics played against the Chicago Wonders in a baseball game sponsored by the Negro Major American and National League Baseball Teams, Inc. Baseball on all levels has been played at the Stadium. It has housed the annual Cleveland school Senate championship baseball game, and in more recent times has been home field to Cleveland State University for many of its baseball contests.

The Stadium became the setting for wild animals and aerial acrobatics in 1950, as the Cole Bros. Circus with Hopalong Cassidy came to town for three performances. For many years the circus had been held in the parking lot adjoining the Stadium, and also at Public Auditorium. This visit to the Stadium drew a crowd of just over 8,000, but a circus show was to be a frequent return visitor in the years ahead.

*The circus played on Cleveland's lakefront for many years, sometimes in the parking lot next to the Stadium, and at other times inside the Stadium itself. A pachyderm parade frequently opened the show.*          *(The Plain Dealer)*

*Baseball players watch and listen as Louis Lane conducts the Cleveland Orchestra in a summer pops concert held just before the start of the ball game. The orchestra played a series of concerts at the Stadium in 1953, and the double treat, music and sport, brought many additional fans to the lakefront.*          *(Musical Arts Association)*

Music was featured at the Stadium in 1953 when the Cleveland Orchestra agreed to schedule its summer "pops concerts" there. The orchestra was housed in a shed in front of the bleachers, and a special sound amplification system was installed for the occasion. An unusual feature of the arrangements that summer was that the orchestra was booked to play on the same nights as the Indians had games scheduled. The concert began at the same time as batting practice. The inaugural concert was held on June 2, with Louis Lane conducting. A crowd of 17,356 showed up for this blend of song and sport. The program consisted of standard pop tunes, with a full orchestral rendering of "Take Me Out to the Ball Game" included for good measure. The critics proclaimed the event musically satisfying. The second half of this "twin-bill" was also deemed a success as the Indians trimmed the Boston Red Sox 7-3.

A musical event of a slightly different order was held on August 14, 1966 when the British Rock group, the Beatles, appeared in concert. That visit was their second to the city. In 1964 they had appeared in Public Auditorium. Over 100,000 Beatles' fans clamored for tickets to that earlier concert, but only 10,000 were able to be admitted to the hall. Their second visit was, therefore, planned for the Stadium so that a much larger audience could be accommodated.

A stage was set up at second base, and a fence was built around the infield. A somewhat disappointing crowd of 24,646 came to see and hear the Beatles at the Stadium. They made up in enthusiasm what they lacked in numbers, as 3,000 of the fans knocked down the fence and clogged the field around the stage. The concert had to be halted for 25 minutes until the security force could get the audience back to its seats. The reason the crowd failed to come up to expectations was never fully understood, although the 1966 experience in Cleveland was not unlike the response in other cities on that year's Beatles' tour.

The City of Cleveland was not overly enthusiastic about rock concerts at either the Stadium or Public Auditorium. Crowd control and the specter of property damage precluded further concerts at the lakefront until the Stadium Corporation took over management.

In 1974 under the sponsorship of Belkin Productions, Inc., the first rock concert was held at the Stadium in what was billed the "World Series of Rock," the most ambitious show of its kind in the midwest. On June 23, Joe Walsh, Lynrd Skynrd, and the Beach Boys entertained a crowd of 32,837. On August 4, a turnout of 34,173 came to hear Emerson, Lake & Palmer. On August 30, a crowd of 81,316 crammed the Stadium to see and hear Crosby, Stills, Nash & Young.

In 1975 four more concerts were held at the Stadium. Chicago headlined one, the Rolling Stones a second, Yes the third, and Faces the fourth. The rock series was postponed in 1976 due to a new field surface having been installed. At rock concerts the field is covered by plywood, and fans occupy the field area as well as the grandstands. It was felt that the newly-laid sod needed more time to root properly, and that admitting concert-goers to the field could have permanently damaged it.

In 1977 the "World Series of Rock" resumed with three concerts. Aerosmith, Pink Floyd, and Peter Frampton drew a total audience of over 193,000 for the three dates. In 1978 the Electric Light Orchestra, the Rolling Stones (their second visit), and Fleetwood Mac appeared. In 1979 Aerosmith returned, and in 1980 Bob Seger headed a rock bill. Altogether, the Stadium has been the site for sixteen rock extravaganzas, with a total audience of 893,000, an average crowd of better than 55,000. The largest crowd for the Series was 82,986, for the Pink Floyd concert on June 25, 1977.

Rock concerts have been a popular Stadium offering since the Stadium Corporation took over the facility's management. Crowds can approach quite near the stage, set up in front of the bleachers (above). The entire field (below) becomes a sea of people for one of the popular events. A plywood surface protects the turf from damage. (The Stadium Corporation)

There have been other varieties of musical presentations at the Stadium as well. In 1975 a polka festival was tried. Twenty bands participated, placed about the perimeter of the field, each with its own dance floor. Bad weather, however, severely curtailed the attendance and only 1,602 turned out. More successful was The World's Greatest Gospel Music Festival, held that same summer, which saw 9,390 assemble for a program of religious song.

However much other kinds of events may seem to dominate the Stadium's schedule, the sacred is a recurring theme. One of the most successful religious events, and the longest, took place July 14-23, 1972, when Evangelist Billy Graham brought his crusade to Cleveland.

When the preacher first saw the Stadium he felt some concern that it might be too large for his purposes, but by the time the Crusade had ended, ten days later, he was very pleased that it had been chosen as the site. Over the span of the Crusade, 372,440 turned out to hear Graham's message and the sounds of a huge choir, with Ethel Waters as featured soloist.

More important to Graham, however, was the fact that 19,608 of those who attended came forward to testify that they were willing to lead new lives for Jesus Christ. Despite one night of severe rain, thunder and lightning, attendance never fell below 25,000, with the largest crowd of the Crusade being slightly above 50,000.

It was an interesting statistic to religious commentators — and to sports buffs as well — that the Crusade drew more people in ten evenings than the Indians had drawn that summer for thirty-seven dates. The Stadium has seemed to be well suited for events of a sacred order.

One other attraction at the Stadium deserves to be mentioned. In 1967 Vernon Stouffer and Gabe Paul (at that time chiefly occupied as executives of the Cleveland Indians baseball team) sponsored a Cleveland entry into the newly formed professional North American Soccer League. They brought over the Stokers from Stoke City, England, to serve as the city's representative during the summer season.

Soccer was played at the Stadium from 1967 through 1969 (in the second and third years sponsored by Howard Metzenbaum and Ted Bonda), but in none of its seasons did it seem to capture the interest of the community. The franchise folded after the 1969 season.

One highlight from the soccer years came on July 10, 1968, when the world famous Pele came to the Stadium to lead his team against the Stokers. A crowd of 16,205 came out to see his exciting style of play. Pele also returned to the Stadium in 1976 for a game between the New York Cosmos and the Dallas Tornado. Fans numbering 14,119 witnessed his second visit.

To mention every event and every thrill that has taken place in the Stadium during its first fifty years would be practically impossible. Hopefully, the sampling of events in this chapter gives a flavor to the wide range of uses that the versatile lakefront facility has enjoyed.

Many and varied as all these events have been, however, the Stadium remains first and foremost the home of the Cleveland Indians and the Cleveland Browns. Their stories come next.

# CHAPTER 5

## *The Indians*

The history of professional baseball in Cleveland goes back to a time long before Cleveland Municipal Stadium was ever considered. In fact, the Stadium is but the sixth home field for the various teams that have been the city's baseball representatives. The first field dates back to 1869.

Cleveland's first professional baseball game was played on June 2 of that year. The Cleveland Forest City's hosted the Cincinnati Red Stockings at Case Commons, a park located at East 38th street, between Scovill and Central avenues. The home team was solidly trounced 25-6.

Cleveland's second baseball field was located at East 55th Street and Garden Street, which became the site for play in 1871. From there the team moved to East 46th Street and Cedar Avenue in 1879, the year in which Cleveland's franchise was admitted into the National League. Cleveland remained in the senior circuit through 1884.

Dropping out of the National League, Cleveland next fielded a team in the American Association in 1887 and 1888. In 1889 the franchise in the National League was renewed. Playing under a new name, the Spiders, the team also had a new owner and a new field. Frank Robison, the owner, was also the holder of a streetcar franchise in the city. He moved his team to a park at East 39th Street and Payne Avenue, right on his trolley line. His choice was calculated to increase the passenger totals for his streetcar business.

The Spiders played competitive ball, and the fans began to show increased support. To accommodate the growing crowds, Robison built a new stadium in 1891. Named League Park, the facility was located at the corner of Lexington Avenue and East 66th Street, between Wade Park and Hough avenues (again, right on a Robison streetcar line).

*League Park, located at East 66th Street and Lexington Avenue, served as the home of Cleveland's major league baseball teams from 1891 until Cleveland Municipal Stadium was built. Even then, it continued as the city's chief baseball park until 1946.   (Cleveland Public Library)*

League Park, the team's fifth home, was to prove a durable one, lasting fifty-five years as the stadium for the city's professional baseball teams. While the city had finally gained a dependable and satisfactory facility, other changes were in the wings for the local baseball club.

Cleveland dropped out of the National league in 1899. In 1900 its baseball future was reorganized when Charles Somers bought the team and secured a franchise for it in the newly-formed American League. Cleveland was one of eight charter members in the new league when it began operations in 1901.

Befitting the team's status in a new league, a new name was called for. The team was called the Blues (sometimes the Bluebirds) after the bright blue uniforms the players wore. In 1902 the name was happily changed to the Broncos. The players, however, did not like that name, so Somers turned to the newspapers for help in running a contest to select a new tag.

The name chosen (effective 1903) was the Naps, selected in honor of the team's star second baseman, Napoleon Lajoie, who the year before had jumped from the National League to the Cleveland team.

The team remained the Naps until 1915 when another newspaper contest was held. This time the Indians was selected as the name. The citizen who submitted the winning entry stated that he had chosen it to honor Luis Francis Sockalexis, a member of the Cleveland club in the late 1890's. He was the first American Indian to play in the major leagues. The name Indians, the sixth nickname for the Cleveland team, has remained. The sixth park, however, Cleveland Municipal Stadium, was still in the future.

One reason for the Stadium's not being built earlier was the fact that League Park was a comfortable and interesting ballpark, with the seats near the playing field. It could handle about 27,000 fans, more than usually attended most of the Indians' home games.

*League Park provided baseball fans with seating close to the field action. The park was limited, however, by its 27,000 capacity and the lack of parking facilities.* (Cleveland Public Library)

*The fabled right field wall at League Park provided many exciting moments for the fans. Only 240 feet from home plate, the wall caused many ricochet shots; good outfield play was of critical importance.  (Cleveland Public Library)*

League Park also provided for some excitement in the way its field dimensions affected play. The left field line stretched 375 feet, and a home run poke would have to sail 460 feet in center. This led to a premium for outfielders as sparkling catches or misplayed drives were certain to provide delight or vexation for the fans. The right field line was a hitter's delight, only 240 feet from home plate. To make a homerun a little more challenging, a 40-foot fence also had to be surmounted in order to clear the bases. The fence, half concrete, half wire, produced a different kind of outfield excitement; fielders had to be able to play the ricochet shot adeptly.

However much people liked League Park (called Dunn Field 1916-1927 after James Dunn who had purchased the team from Somers in 1916 for $500,000), it did have some obvious limitations. It was completely boxed in by neighboring buildings. It could not accommodate a really large crowd, and parking was nearly non-existent. It was because of these factors that E. S. Barnard, who operated the team for Jim Dunn's widow from 1922 to 1927, was active in promoting plans for the new facility on the lakefront.

So, all the while the Stadium plans were being formulated, it was generally assumed that the Indians would abandon League Park and become permanent tenants at the Stadium.

The Stadium's opening year came and went, and the Indians continued to play at League Park. The new owner, Alva Bradley, who had purchased the team from Dunn's estate for $1,000,000 in 1927, refused to sign a lease with the city until he was sure that the team's interests were fully protected.

After months of negotiations, a lease was finally agreed upon. The Indians' first game at Cleveland Municipal Stadium was set for Sunday, July 31, 1932 against the Philadelphia Athletics. Lefty Grove (later inducted into the baseball Hall of Fame) took the mound for Philadelphia, and Mel Harder (who would go on to win 223 games pitching for the Indians, later serving as their pitching coach for many seasons) was picked to start for the Indians. At the time Wes Farrell was the Tribe's ace pitcher, but he complained of back trouble, so Harder got the nod. Crowds of people left home early to view the inaugural game. By the time the game was due to start the crowd had grown to number 80,184 (the largest crowd ever to have assembled for a major league baseball game). The fans were not disappointed in the kind of game they saw. After a superb pitching duel, the Athletics, unfortunately, came out on the better side, 1-0.

The Indians continued to play at Municipal Stadium during 1932, and spent the entire 1933 season there. At the conclusion of that season, Indians' management studied the attendance figures for the year. A total

of 387,936 had paid their way into the Stadium, a drop of about 80,000 from the previous year, and almost 100,000 below the team's last full year at League Park in 1931. The Indians finished 1933 in fourth place for the fourth consecutive year; their record had fallen below the .500 mark, and the Stadium was blamed.

Batting averages for the team had plummeted at the Stadium without the aid of a friendly right field wall, and with less offense, Cleveland had its worst won-lost record in five years. President Alva Bradley had seen enough of the Stadium, and he brought his team back to League Park for the 1934 season.

In 1935 the Stadium was the scene for the then-new annual baseball classic, the All-Star Game between the American and National Leagues' outstanding players. The Cleveland game was the third in the series, and a crowd of 69,831 came to the lakefront for it. They witnessed the American League win its third consecutive game, this time by a 4-1 score. Cleveland's Mel Harder pitched three innings for the AL squad and earned a save.

In 1935 Cleveland Municipal Stadium hosted the first of its baseball All-Star Games. That contest drew 69,831 fans to the ball park and established the all-time attendance record for the summer classic. Programs for the game sold for 25 cents. (Osborne Engineering Company)

The Stadium became a secondary place for the Indians to play in these years. It was the choice for home games whenever it seemed as though the crowd might be likely to exceed League Park's seating capacity.

A good example of this dual park scheduling took place in 1937 when the Great Lakes Exposition was decorating the lakefront. The Indians that year offered a special attraction. For an extra 25 cents, fans could buy a ticket which not only admitted them to the baseball game, but also would allow them onto the fair grounds as well. The promotion was a success. In ten dates under this plan, the Tribe drew 276,788 spectators. The entire year's attendance totaled 564,849, their best draw since

1926.

The typical schedule of the Indians in these times was for them to play Sunday games and doubleheaders at the Stadium, and the rest of the schedule at League Park. In 1939, however, an innovation was decided upon: night baseball! Now the Stadium had one more point in its favor, as League Park was without lights.

The first night game was played June 27, 1939, against the Detroit Tigers. Bob Feller, who the previous year had thrilled the baseball world by striking out eighteen Tigers in

Detroit, took the mound for the Indians. He carved out a masterful performance, hurling a one-hit shutout as the Indians won 5-0 before 53,305.

Bob Feller was probably the greatest gate attraction that the Indians ever had, and one of the greatest in the major leagues during his prime. He came to the Indians in 1936, signed by super scout Cy Slapnicka, without ever having played one game of minor league baseball. In 18 years with the Indians he won 266 games while losing only 162. The figures are deceiving, though, because when the United States became involved in World War II, Feller enlisted in the armed services. He missed the entire 1942, 1943, and 1944 seasons, and almost

*Bob Feller, who joined the Indians in 1936, became one of baseball's greatest gate attractions. His brilliant pitching kept turnstiles clicking at the Stadium and around the league. Feller retired in 1956 and was inducted into the Baseball Hall of Fame in 1962. (Cleveland Indians)*

all of 1945. The year before he enlisted he had won 25 games; in 1946, his first full season back, he notched 26 victories, while striking out 348 opposing batters. Had his pitching career not been interrupted, his statistics would surely have been even more impressive. Nonetheless, through his last season in 1956, he brought countless thrills to baseball fans in Cleveland and throughout the league. Feller was selected as a member of the Hall of Fame in 1962, his first year of eligibility.

If Bob Feller had a rival at the box office, it was the New York Yankee star, Joe DiMaggio. Cleveland Stadium played a role in his most famous accomplishment.

In 1941 the "Yankee Clipper," as he was nicknamed, set his major league record for a consecutive game hitting streak. His streak began on May 15 and had reached 55 games when the Yankees arrived in Cleveland. The first game in the series, played at League Park, was no problem for DiMaggio as he connected for three hits in four at-bats.

The second game in the series was played at the Stadium, a night contest on July 17, 1941. DiMaggio's streak had captured the interest of the fans, and the largest crowd ever to come out for a night game, 67,468, was in the park. Al Smith was the starting pitcher for Cleveland. He faced the "Clipper" three times, walking him once. The other two times, brilliant defensive plays by third-baseman Ken Keltner nipped DiMaggio at first base. Jim Bagby faced DiMaggio in the eighth inning, with one out and the bases filled with Yankees. He induced DiMaggio to ground a ball to shortstop Lou Boudreau, who converted the shot into a rally-killing double play. The great hitting streak — 56 games — came to an end at Municipal Stadium.

*Bill Veeck (right) bought the Indians in 1946 and ushered in some of the most exciting years in the team's history. It was his decision to move the club to the Stadium on a permanent basis starting with the 1947 season. Here he looks on as Lou Boudreau signs a new contract as the Indians' manager. (Cleveland Indians)*

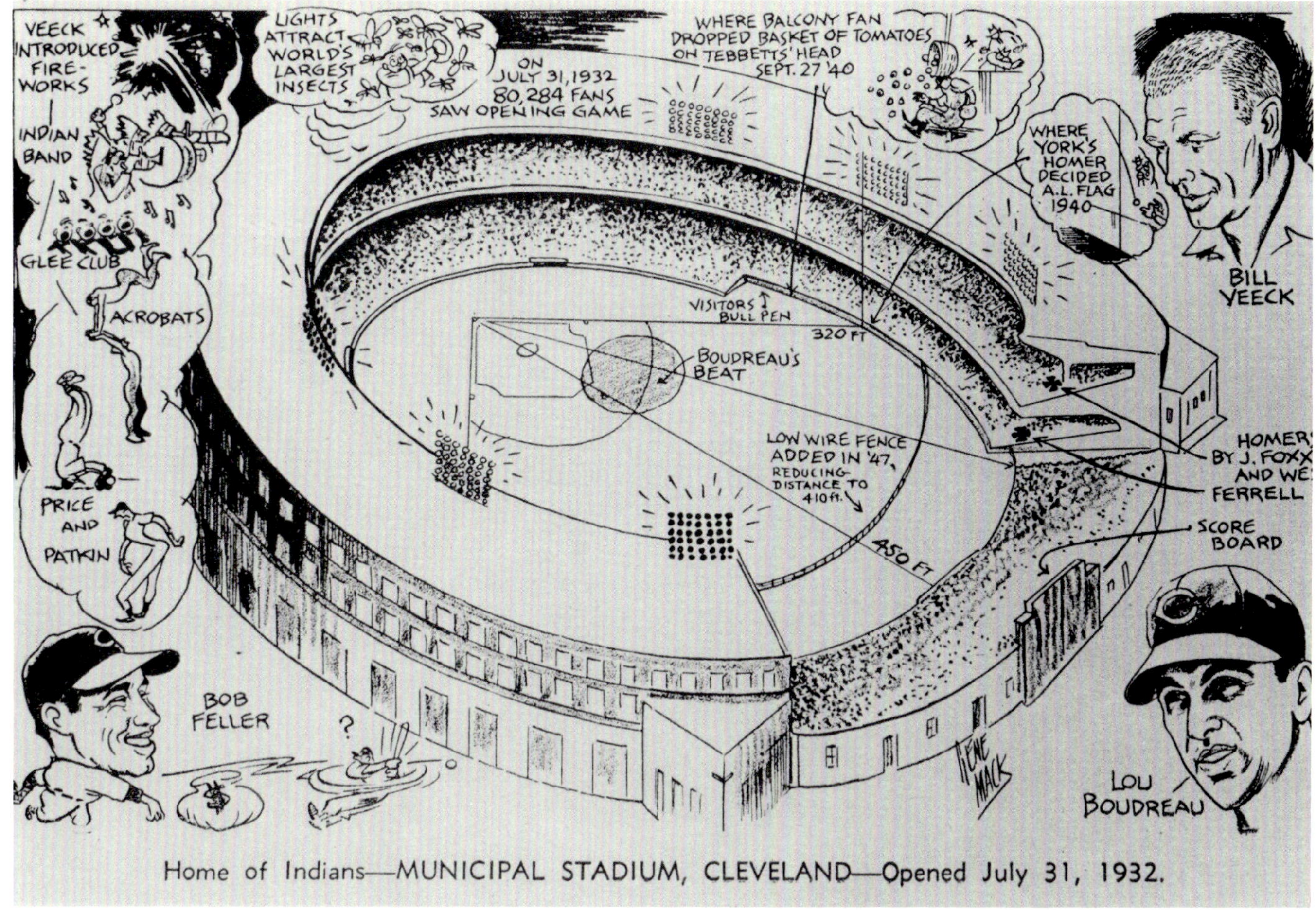


*The colorful years of Bill Veeck's ownership brought a phenomenal surge of fan support. This cartoon, originally published in The **Sporting News**, depicts some Stadium highlights.* (University of Notre Dame Archives)

The World War II years were not good ones for baseball. With so many of its stars away in service, attendance lagged. This created an opening for an exciting era for the Indians. On June 21, 1946 Bill Veeck bought controlling interest in the Indians from Alva Bradley. (It was at this time that comedian Bob Hope, who grew up in Cleveland, also bought his shares in the franchise).

Wounded in the war, Veeck was hobbled by his injuries and often in considerable pain. Yet he was on the go, speaking anywhere he could, to boost the Indians with the public. He would even rove through the park during ballgames, just to talk to the spectators. Confident of the team's future (for the first time the Tribe had drawn over 1,000,000 fans in 1946), Veeck negotiated a lease with the City of Cleveland that would make the Stadium the Indians' permanent home starting with the 1947 baseball season. The last game at old League Park was played September 21, 1946.

One of the first innovations made by Bill Veeck was to install a fence across the Stadium outfield. His conversations with the fans had convinced him that the home run ball was one of their chief thrills. So before the 1947 season began, a 5-1/2 foot high fence was installed. It greatly cheered Cleveland **Press** sports editor Whitey Lewis who had campaigned for the fence for years, believing that it would make games at the Stadium more exciting.

Veeck was an innovator and a daring man. Under his sponsorship in 1947 the first black ballplayer in the American League was called up by the Indians. Larry Doby, who was to star for many years for the Indians, eased the way to equal opportunity for other black athletes in the American League.

One of the highlights of 1947 occurred on July 10, when Indian pitcher Don Black tossed the first no-hit game in Stadium history, as Cleveland beat the Athletics 3-0. It was the high point in his career and crowned his victory over a series of personal problems that had plagued him.

Ironically, that year was also one of tragedy for Black. On September 13, as he stepped to the plate for his turn in the batting order, he suddenly reeled dizzily as his world went dark. While standing at the plate he had been struck down by a cerebral hemmorage. Black battled back in the months ahead, and even managed to pitch again the following season. But it was never to be the same for him; after a few innings in 1948, his major league career came to an end.

If there is any one year that stands out in Cleveland's baseball history, it would have to be 1948. What a year it was — both on the field and at the turnstiles. The Indians set a major league record for attendance that year when 2,620,627 fans paid their way into the Stadium. That record stood as the major league mark until 1962 when the Los Angeles Dodgers (of the National League) drew 2,755,184. Cleveland continued to hold the American League record until 1980, when on the very last day of the season, it was eclipsed by the New York Yankees' total of 2,627,417.

Crowds of 60,000-70,000 were almost commonplace that year as the city was infected with "Pennant Fever."

The 1948 Indians were a team that brought thrills with exciting fielding plays and a potent attack. Led by their shortstop-manager, Lou Boudreau, who had been named playing manager for the 1942 season at the remarkable age of 24, the infield sparkled.

Boudreau batted .355 that year and was named the league's Most Valuable Player. Ken Keltner held down third base and contributed a .297 batting average and 31 homeruns. At second base was Joe Gordon, who batted .280, while driving in 124 runs and stroking 32 homers.

*Lou Boudreau, the Indians' manager-shortstop during the 1948 championship season, was always very popular with the fans. Because of his contributions to Cleveland baseball, the roadway adjoining the Stadium was dedicated Boudreau Boulevard in his honor.*          (Cleveland Indians)

The 1948 Cleveland Indians drew 2,620,627 fans to the Stadium and brought the city its second World Series championship. Crowds of 60,000 were commonplace that year to watch a team that offered excitement at bat, in the field, and from the pitching mound. (Cleveland Indians)

Larry Doby starred in centerfield and contributed a .301 average. In left field was Dale Mitchell who cracked the ball at a .336 pace.

The pitching staff was a solid one, with Feller, Gene Bearden, and Bob Lemon the staff mainstays. The mound crew was also bolstered by the mid-season addition of the fabled Satchel Paige who added more to the team than the six victories he recorded in the stretch run.

Despite the power and pitching, the Indians found themselves in a tight pennant race where each game really counted. Perhaps the single most thrilling moment of an unforgettable season came on August 8, in the first game of a doubleheader against the Yankees. Lou Boudreau had been injured a few games earlier in a collision at second base and had scratched himself from the lineup, hampered by a strained right shoulder and a sprained left ankle. The Indians were two runs down in the seventh inning, but they had the bases loaded with two out. The 73,844 fans rose to their feet with a roar as they saw Boudreau limp from the dugout, bat in hand, to pinch hit. Sure enough, Boudreau delivered, a single past the shortstop, to tie the game. The Indians went on to win the game — and the doubleheader. It was that kind of magic year. The magic notwithstanding, when the final game of the regular season was completed, the Indians found themselves in a tie for first place with the Boston Red Sox. A one-game playoff was ordered, to be played in Boston. The Tribe was ready; they clobbered the Red Sox before a stunned Fenway Park crowd, 8-3, behind the five-hit pitching of Gene Bearden and the two-homerun support of Boudreau.

The Indians had made it to the World Series for the first time since 1920. There they had to face Boston's National League club, the Braves. The series opened in Boston with the teams splitting a pair of games (Cleveland's loss being a 1-0 defeat in which the winning run scored after a heated dispute about Bob Feller's pickoff attempt at second base).

The next three games were held at the Stadium, with the Indians taking two of them and setting another attendance record in the third game of the set; 86,288 turned out, hoping to see the team win the Series. (The National League later set a new record for a World Series game when the Dodgers drew 92,706 to the Los Angeles Coliseum October 6, 1959). Unfortunately, the Braves won and forced a return to Boston for the sixth game. Cleveland won that game, and thus the Series. A crowd of over 300,000 lined

two million figure. That year also brought another change in team ownership. A group headed by Ellis Ryan bought the team midway through the season from Bill Veeck. The Tribe ended in third place.

In 1950 the Indians slipped another notch, dropping to fourth place despite a fine 92-62 won-lost record. One of the highlights of that year was the longest home run ever hit in the Stadium. On June 23 Luke Easter, Tribe first baseman, powered a ball into the upper deck of Section 4, a

*Cleveland surrendered its baseball title in 1949. On the last day of the season the crown which had adorned the Indian mascot above Stadium Gate A was taken down. The Indians finished in third place. (Cleveland Indians)*

downtown streets as the Indians were welcomed home as World Champions of 1948.

The following year was another fine year for attendance. The Indians' draw of 2,233,771 marks the second time in the team's history that attendance passed the

distance of 477 feet from home plate. (No ball has ever been hit into the bleachers, although Mickey Mantle, Frank Howard, and Rocky Colavito all have hit homers which bounced near the bleacher wall in left center, a distance of some 465 feet from the plate.

*Al Lopez took over the managerial reins of the Tribe in 1951. In six years as manager he never piloted the team to a finish lower than second place. He is generally regarded as having been the Indians' most successful field leader.*　　　　　(Cleveland Indians)

A new manager arrived in Cleveland for the 1951 season; Al Lopez was to lead the team for six years, and spark its third league championship in 1954. Under his guidance, the Tribe finished second five times, and first once.

In 1952 the Indians opened a Cleveland Hall of Fame off the Stadium's main concourse to honor those greats who had worn a Cleveland uniform. The following players were eventually inducted: Steve O'Neill, Cy Young, Mel Harder, Bob Feller, Bob Lemon, Hal Trosky, Nap Lajoie, Kenny Keltner, Bill Bradley, Lou Boudreau, Joe Sewell, Joe Jackson, Earl Averill, Tris Speaker, Satchel Paige, Jim Hegan, Elmer Flick, Larry Doby, and Stan Coveleskie. The popular shrine was removed in 1972, with the mementoes being transferred to the Ohio Baseball Museum in Springfield.

In 1953 the team was sold once more, coming under the leadership of Myron H. Wilson. His investment was soon to be rewarded by the excitement of 1954 when the Indians set an American League record by winning 111 games. (The National League record of 116 was set by Chicago in 1906).

In 1954 the Indians had a great pitching staff. The staff consisted of the big four starters: Feller, Bob Lemon, Early Wynn, and Mike Garcia, with Art Houtteman the fifth man. The bullpen consisted of Art Hoskins, Bob Hooper, Hal Newhouser, the great veteran from Detroit, and two rookie stars, Don Mossi and Ray Narleski. For the season, this staff not only won 111 games, but also posted a team earned-run average of 2.78!

The 1954 Cleveland Indians established the American League all-time record for most victories with 111. Below first baseman Vic Wertz, flanked by Manager Al Lopez and general manager Hank Greenberg, testifies to the team's winning the American League pennant.     (Cleveland Indians)

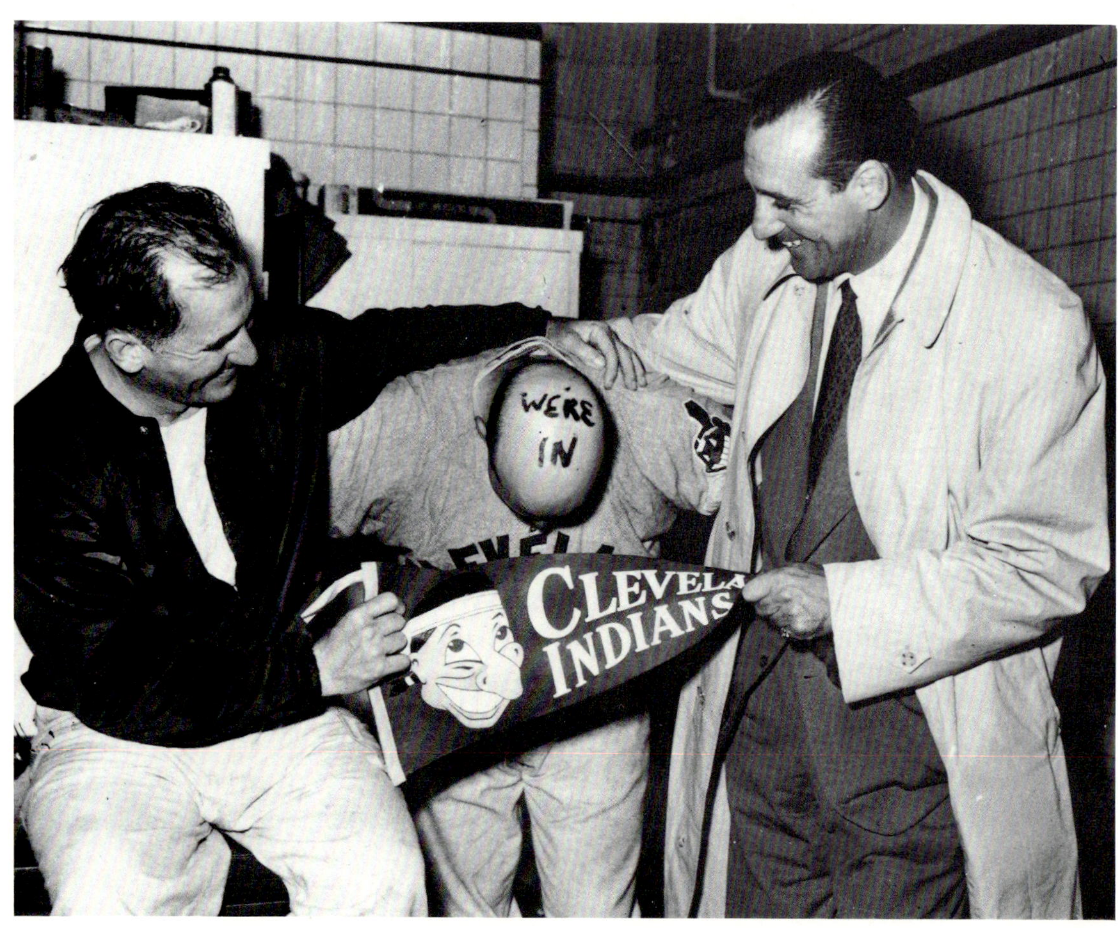

The team had offensive clout as well. Second baseman Bobby Avila had his best year with a league-leading .341 batting average. Third baseman Al Rosen (chosen the 1953 MVP on the basis of 43 home runs and 145 RBIs) hit 24 homers and drove in 102 runs while hitting an even .300. Larry Doby contributed 32 home runs and 126 runs batted in, and newcomer Vic Wertz contributed to the team's power after he arrived here from Baltimore.

It was not as exciting a year as 1948 had been. In the previous years, the Indians had accustomed the fans to seeing good baseball, but also to seeing the team fade into second place. Attendance for the year totaled only 1,335,472. One attendance record was set, however. On September 12 the largest crowd in the major leagues ever to watch a doubleheader, 84,587, saw the Indians whip the Yankees in both games.

The World Series of 1954 is one that most Cleveland fans remember with frustration. The pitching staff which had performed so well during the season did not have the same touch in the Series. The New York Giants, led by the hitting of Dusty Rhodes, captured the Series in four straight games. That Series also featured Willie Mays' famed catch: while racing with his back toward home plate, he snared a mighty wallop off the bat of Vic Wertz, robbing the Indians of their chance for a first game victory (that catch was at the Polo Grounds, not the Stadium).

In 1954 Cleveland also hosted its second All-Star game. On July 13 the game was played before a crowd of 68,751, the second highest attendance ever to view the classic. The American League won in a slugfest, 11-9.

Cleveland held on to second place in 1955 and 1956. In 1956 it was believed that a key to the future had been found in an outstanding young pitcher. Herb Score, a left-handed hurler with impressive credentials, improved on his 1955 rookie season record of 16-10 with a 20-9 mark in 1956, striking out 263 batters while establishing a 2.53 earned run average.

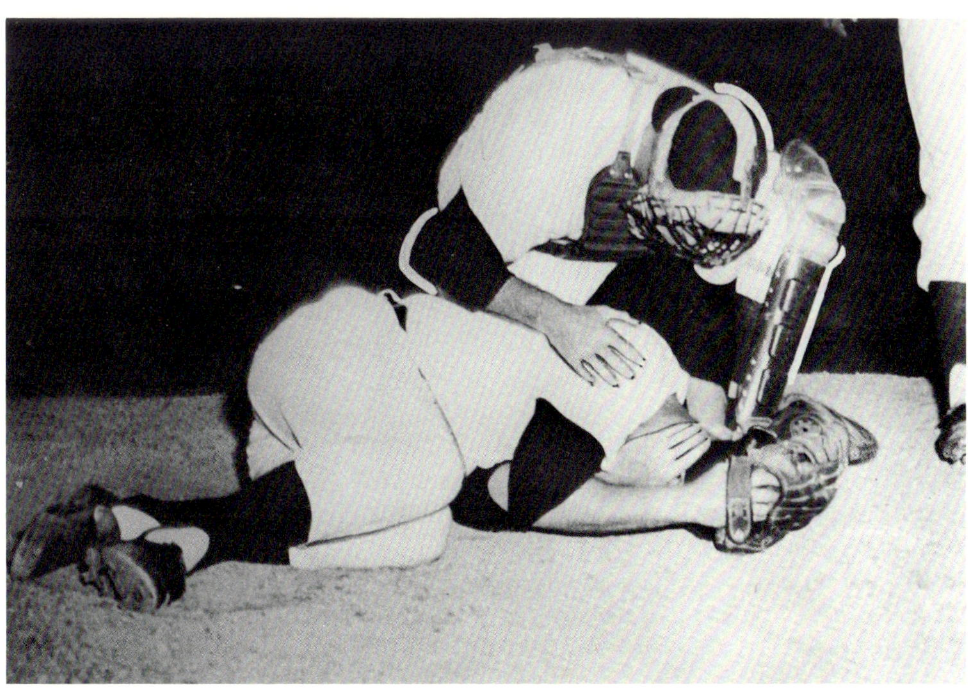

*The Indians' talented southpaw hurler, Herb Score, is down on the mound after being struck in the eye by a line drive. The injury curtailed a promising career, but Score has remained a popular figure with Clevelanders as the Tribe's veteran radio voice.     (The Cleveland Press)*

Score began 1957 in great style, fanning 39 batters in 36 innings. Then tragedy struck. The Yankees were in town. Score was on the mound, and Gil McDougald was at bat. McDougald lined one of Score's pitches right back at him; before he could react, the ball had struck him in the eye. The young pitcher was carried from the field on a stretcher. Score recovered, returned to the team in 1958, and pitched until 1962, but the promise of a great career can be said to have ended on that fateful May 8 evening.

In 1956 the ownership of the club changed once more. William R. Daley became chief stockholder for an investment of $3,961,800. Wilson stayed on as president, however, until 1963.

In 1958 Frank Lane was appointed the Tribe's general manager, and an era of player trading began. In 1959 the Indians pulled back into second place, but just as the 1960 season was due to open, Lane traded the very popular Rocky Colavito to Detroit. Not since the Indians started play in the Stadium had there been a trade which so enraged and alienated the fans. The Indians dropped into fourth place, and attendance plummeted by over a half million fans.

The 1960s were not years of prosperity for the Tribe, either in the standings or at the gate. Attendance never hit the million mark, and the best finish they managed was third place in 1968.

In 1961 Gabe Paul, who had built the successful teams in Cincinnati, arrived in Cleveland as general manager. He bought controlling interest in the team in 1962 and served as the Indians' president until 1971.

*Gabe Paul came to the Indians' front office in 1961 from the Cincinnati Reds. In all but five years since that time (when he served as the New York Yankees' president) he has headed the Tribe's front office. (Cleveland Indians)*

The 1960s were not without thrills for baseball fans, because there were many memorable moments at the Stadium. In 1963 the city hosted its third All-Star game with a crowd of 44,160 attending. On July 31 that year, the scoreboard ran out of fireworks when four Indians, Woodie Held, Tito Francona, Larry Brown, and Pedros Ramos, hit back-to-back homeruns. There was also the pride of seeing Early Wynn return to Cleveland and notch his 300th career victory.

In 1972 a new regime took over control of the team. Nick Mileti, who owned the city's professional basketball and hockey teams, added the Indians to his sports empire, serving as general partner in the new ownership.

Since the events on the field were not always the most satisfying to the fans, management tried to find added avenues for entertaining the faithful. Promotions of a wide variety were held, particularly under the presidencies of Mileti and Alva T. Bonda (who took over in 1975).

Promotions (or "stunts" as baseball purists might term them) were not just a recent phenomenon. Bill Veeck had been a master, providing all kinds of giveaways. He even held one night for the "ordinary fan," where one lucky patron went home laden down with prizes.

One of the most famous of Veeck's stunts in Cleveland was the hiring of baseball magician Jackie Price. Price was more of an acrobat than anything else. He could throw three balls with one motion, bat upside down, and hit a high pop fly, race

under it in a jeep and make a catch. He provided the fans with many good laughs.

Promotions have ranged from the more conservative, such as old-timer games, bat or helmet days (in which children receive a premium) to the hiring of an act to perform during or after a game. Some of the acts hired by the Indians have been real daredevils.

In 1974 Hugo Zucchini was blasted out of a cannon. In 1975 money was strewn about the infield and the contestants were given 90 seconds to scramble for it. The famous Karl Wallenda also did his balancing act in the Stadium in both years. A wire was stretched across the field, 115 feet above the ground, and stretching about 700 feet in length. Wallenda then walked across, from one end to the other. When he reached the middle of his journey, he paused, did a headstand, and then continued safely to the other side. Wallenda stated that the toughest part of his Stadium stunt was coping with the wind, an added element of danger. The walk across the tightrope took about fifteen minutes.

Taking Wallenda's feat one step further into danger, in 1977 the Vashek Duo did a motorcycle stunt high above the field. Vashek rode a motorcycle on a cable across the field while his wife swung from a trapeze suspended below the cycle!

Then there was A. J. Bakunas. He leaped from the Stadium roof onto an inflated nylon bag which measured 18 feet by 25 feet. The velocity of his fall was about 96 miles per hour.

Promotions are an integral part of baseball. One of the most popular of such events is the old-timers game. Above, four of Cleveland's great pitchers, (from left) Bob Lemon, Mike Garcia, Early Wynn, and Bob Feller, return for a 1966 game. Bat day (below) probably ranks as the most successful of all promotions; here thousands of youngsters testify to their pleasure with the annual giveaway at the Stadium.     (Cleveland Indians)

One Stadium stunt featured a man who entertained the fans, whisking himself about the Stadium by means of a rocket pack strapped to his back. Promotions have featured many varieties of daredevil artistry.                    (Cleveland Indians)

One promotion did not turn out the way it had been hoped. On June 4, 1974, 25,134 fans turned out for "Beer Night," at which the brew was specially priced. Too much beer was consumed by some of the fans, and a riot broke out in the bottom of the ninth inning as the Indians were battling the Texas Rangers. The Indians had tied the score and there were two men on base when the intoxicated fans burst from the stands and swarmed about the field. Some might have been motivated by the brawl that had occurred between the two teams the previous week in Texas, but most were just carried away by the effects of the brew. The umpires and Stadium police were unable to restore order, and the game was declared forfeit to Texas. The incident is a smudge on the otherwise grand history of the Stadium.

As part of baseball's tribute to the nation's bicentennial celebration in 1976, fans in each city were asked to vote for the most memorable moment of baseball in their city. Cleveland fans selected an event that took place on April 8, 1975. (The previous October 10, Frank Robinson had been named playing-manager of the Indians, the first black ever to be named to manage a major league club). That cold spring day, the Indians opened their home season against the Yankees. Robinson, in his very first time at bat as manager, stroked a Doc Medich pitch over the fence for a homerun. The Stadium came alive, fully appreciating the significance of that swing — the most memorable in Indians' history.

Cleveland fans voted that the most memorable baseball event at the Stadium was Frank Robinson's homerun in his very first at bat as Cleveland Indians' manager. Here he is seen being congratulated by John Lowenstein for his thrilling debut. (Paul Tepley)

Gaylord Perry mystified opposing batters and delighted Cleveland fans in his years with the Indians. Always suspected of "doctoring" the baseball, here Gaylord is checked out by the umpire for any "illegal substances." (Paul Tepley)

No-hitters always provide fans with a thrill. Here Dick Bosman is congratulated by his teammates after hurling a 4-0 masterpiece against the Oakland A's on July 19, 1974. (Paul Tepley)

Baseball excitement became plentiful in 1979. Though the Indians did not manage to win consistently, the team did succeed in capturing the fans' enthusiasm, and attendance began to improve. Here second baseman Duane Kuiper prepares to land after firing a double play relay to first base.     (Paul Tepley)

Clevelanders have established that they will support baseball in a tremendous way. All it will take is a winning team and exciting play. In 1978 the team changed ownership yet again with F. J. O'Neill, a civic leader, buying majority interest. He brought Gabe Paul back to Cleveland from New York as team president. Paul has often referred to Cleveland as a "sleeping giant," a city that will just go wild with the right team.

With their return, new money was pumped into the franchise, and new talent was brought to the team. Despite ending both the 1979 and 1980 seasons in sixth place, the Indians played some exciting baseball, and the fans found some new heroes to cheer. One man in particular has won the fans' affections as no other player has since Rocky Colavito. Joe Charboneau, who was named the American League Rookie of the Year for 1980, has attracted quite a following.

In both 1979 and 1980 more than a million fans turned out to watch the Indians play. Clearly they are hungry for a winner. When that appears likely to happen, Cleveland can be grateful that it has the Stadium to handle the number of fans that will storm the lakefront.

From 1947, the year that the Stadium became the Tribe's permanent home, through 1980, the Indians have drawn a total attendance of 35,694,057 fans, for a yearly average attendance of 1,049,825.

In those same years they have finished as follows: first place, twice; second place, six times; third place, twice; fourth place, seven times; fifth place, seven times; sixth place, nine times; (never seventh) and eighth place, once. Their median finish is thus part way between fourth and fifth place, and yet they have averaged over a million fans a year.

In 1981 in recognition of the support which the city has given baseball and of the Stadium's golden anniversary, Cleveland was named to host its fourth All-Star game. Washington, D.C. is the only other major league franchise to have hosted the game that many times.

The "sleeping giant" stirred in 1979 and 1980. When a winner returns to the Stadium there is no doubt that Cleveland will once again prove to the baseball world that, no longer asleep, it is truly a giant in the sport.

*Joe Charboneau, American League rookie of the year in 1980, established himself as Cleveland's most popular ball player since Rocky Colavito. He has played a major role in rekindling the hopes of the city for a winning ball club. (Cleveland Indians)*

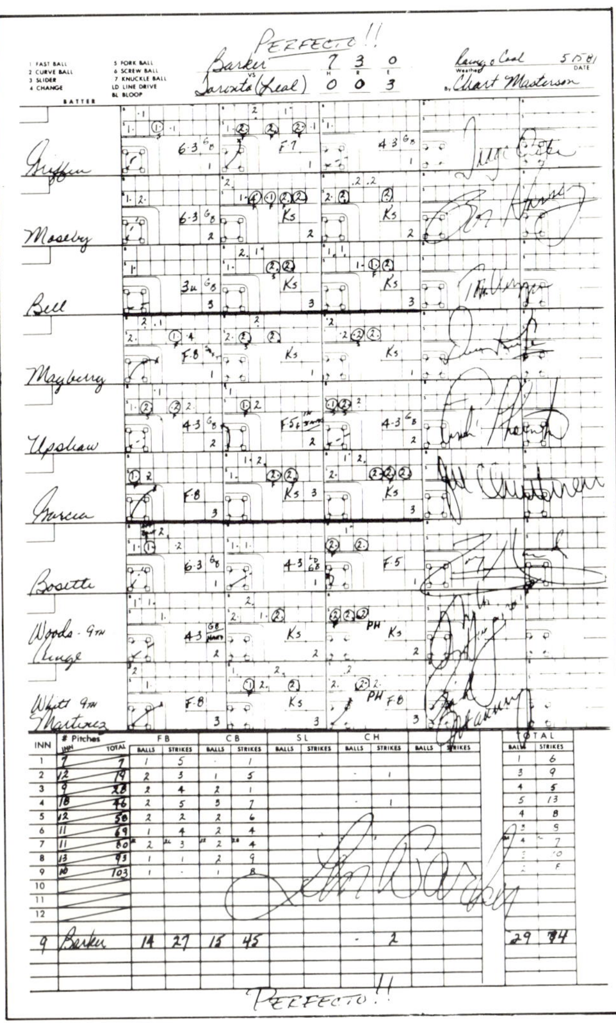

Perhaps the greatest individual baseball accomplishment at the Stadium took place on May 15, 1981. Pitching against the Toronto Blue Jays, Len Barker hurled the first perfect game in Stadium history. This was only the 11th perfect game ever in major league baseball and the first by an Indian since 1908.

As an indication of Barker's total dominance, the Indians' official pitching chart (left) shows that he threw 74 strikes and only 29 balls, 41 fastballs and 60 curves, and didn't reach a three ball count on any batter. The chart was made into a plaque for Barker after it was signed by all the Indians who played in the game: Jorge Orta, Ron Hassey, Tom Veryzer, Duane Kuiper, Andre Thornton, Joe Charboneau, Toby Harrah, Mike Hargrove and Rick Manning.

A Barker trademark is his high leg kick (right) as he pitches to John Mayberry.		(Cleveland Indians, Paul Tepley)

Depicted here are scenes from the two most exciting championship games in Cleveland Browns' history. Lou Groza (above) kicked this 16-yard field goal with 20 seconds on the clock to beat the Los Angeles Rams in 1950. Below, Jim Brown cracks the Baltimore Colts' line in Cleveland's 1964 victory. Before, between, and since these moments, the Browns have provided countless other thrills for Stadium fans.

*(Stadium Corporation)*

# CHAPTER 6

## *The Browns*

The Cleveland Browns have been the city's football representatives for so many years that many fans have forgotten that this is only the most recent Cleveland professional football team.

Cleveland's participation in organized professional football dates back to 1920, the era in which the National Football League (called the American Professional Football Association until 1922) was undergoing organization. The formation of the new league was meant to provide some order and degree of meaningful competition in what was then considered a club sport.

Cleveland fielded a team in the new league for two years, 1920-1921, under the name of the Indians. The Cleveland franchise, like so many of those in that formative period, did not last. The city was without a representative in 1922. The Indians were reorganized in 1923, but once again the team could not make it financially (they were 3-1-3 that season).

In 1924 Cleveland benefitted at the expense of its neighbor to the south when the Canton Bulldogs were moved to Cleveland to take advantage of a larger potential audience. The 1924 Cleveland Bulldogs were an exciting team, finishing with a 7-1-1 record at the top of the circuit.

In 1926 Cleveland left behind the National Football League and fielded a team in the newly-formed rival organization, the American Football League. Their entry into the new association was named the Panthers. The Panthers achieved a 3-2 record in the new league, but the financial resources were not there. The league folded after just one season of play.

In 1927 Cleveland was back in the NFL with another Bulldog team, but it too lasted only one year. The city was then without a professional team until 1931, when another attempt was made in the NFL with a third Indians team; it played to a 2-8 record and folded after that one season. The 1931 Indians, however, earned a page in Stadium history by being the first professional team to play there (winning an exhibition game as explained in Chapter 4).

It was not until 1936 that Cleveland again had a football team. In that year another new league was formed, once again called the American Football League, and Cleveland had an entry which was named the Rams. The team finished the season with a 5-2-2 record, good enough for second place.

The success of the team prompted some reorganization, and new management brought it into the older and better established NFL in 1937. Competition was considerably tougher in the older circuit, and the Rams dropped to a 1-10 record, while playing their home games at League Park. The next season, the Rams' record showed improvement, but attendance at League Park averaged only about 5,000 fans per game.

In order to try to stimulate greater support from the fans, the Rams decided to move their home games to the Stadium for the 1939 season. There they played .500 ball and drew considerably better, the worst crowd numbering 6,085 and their best totalling 25,696.

Dan Reeves was the owner of the Cleveland Rams. After battling several years with the problems of poor attendance, he announced in January, 1946 that he was moving his team to Los Angeles.    (The Cleveland Press)

The 1945 edition of the Cleveland Rams listens to its coach's instructions as fall workouts get underway. The team went on to bring the city its first NFL championship since the 1924 Bulldogs' first place finish.    (The Cleveland Press)

The Rams continued to make the Stadium their home, playing thirteen games there over the next three years. In 1943 Rams' owner Dan Reeves asked for permission to fold the team due to his own service in the military, and also due to the diminishing supply of football talent. (Similar problems affected the other teams as well, with the Pittsburgh Steelers and the Philadelphia Eagles playing as a merged team that year with the nickname "Steagles").

In 1944 the Rams were reactivated but returned to League Park. In 1945 League Park was also the site for some games. It was a year in which the Rams, behind the fine quarterbacking of rookie Bob Waterfield, were moving toward a title. As they approached nearer their goal, attendance peaked, and a large crowd turned out to watch them at League Park on November 11, 1945. Temporary seating had been added to accommodate the crowd, but overcrowding led to trouble. The weight and movement of the fans caused the stands to separate from the base and give way. Thirty-one spectators were injured in the collapse.

The Rams went on to win their division, and a championship game was scheduled for Cleveland against the Washington Redskins. Because of the seating fiasco at League Park, and because the Stadium was able to handle a much larger crowd, the championship game was played on the lakefront.

It was a bitterly cold day, with temperatures plummeting to the zero degree mark as the Rams and Redskins took the field. In order to keep the playing surface as suitable as possible, it had been covered with straw and a tarpaulin. The frigid temperatures also affected attendance, as only 32,178 fans were present. They saw an exciting game, with Cleveland edging the visitors 15-14.

Cleveland had won its first football championship game. While the city was still celebrating the victory, Rams' owner Dan Reeves made an announcement that numbed the fans. On January 12, 1946, he informed the community that he was moving the team to Los Angeles. The city reacted as though it had been betrayed, but the financial facts were clear. Even in the championship season the Rams had lost money, operating almost $40,000 in the red. Cleveland had not really supported the Rams.

The city's sense of loss at the Rams' departure was diminished by the knowledge that a new team would be playing that fall. In 1944 plans for a new football league had been announced, the All-American Football Conference. Cleveland was slated to receive one of the franchises. Undoubtedly this information had also helped Reeves make his decision to move the Rams. From the very start of the new league, the local newspapers had given the AAFC as much attention as was being given to the established team.

Arthur B. McBride was the owner of the new Cleveland franchise, one of eight teams in the new circuit. To select a name for the team, he turned to the traditional method of a newspaper contest. The name selected at first was the Panthers. It was then rejected as having been the property of an earlier team and one which had not fared well. The second choice was to name the team after a winner.

One of the real winners of the time was heavyweight boxing champion, Joe Louis, nicknamed the "Brown Bomber." The name was shortened to just the "Browns." It so happened that this was also the name of the team's coach, Paul Brown, who agreed with the choice after some persuasion.

Brown was not unknown to Cleveland football fans. He had started his coaching career in high school ball in Ohio. He led the famous Massillon High School Tigers to many triumphs. He then moved on to serve as head coach of the Ohio State University Buckeyes, where he met with more success. In the war years he coached for the Great Lakes Academy team. Coach Brown brought his winning tradition to Cleveland with him.

The Browns opened their first season at the Stadium, hosting Miami in a night game. From the very first the Browns were accepted by the fans as none of their predecessors had been. A crowd of 60,135 turned out to see the Browns earn their first victory, a 44-0 rout of the visitors. At that time it was the largest crowd anywhere in the nation to witness a professional football game.

The 1946 Browns were a delight to the Cleveland fans. They won 12 of their 14 games, outscoring their opponents 423-137, and defeating the New York Yankees in the championship game.
(Cleveland Browns)

*The early Browns' teams were rich in talent. Marion Motley (upper left), Dante Lavelli (upper right), Otto Graham (bottom left) and Bill Willis (bottom right) all contributed to the team's early successes. All four of the players were later inducted into the Pro Football Hall of Fame.* (Cleveland Browns)

The Browns' winning story continued.
Cleveland dominated the league. Paul
Brown had put together a great team. He
had signed Otto Graham as his quarterback
and provided him with great receivers in
Dante Lavelli and Mac Speedie. In the
backfield Marion Motley was a standout;
Bill Willis was an all-star at guard, and Lou
Groza at tackle. Today, Lavelli, Graham,
Groza, Willis and Motley are all enshrined
in the Pro Football Hall of Fame in Canton,
Ohio, as is Paul Brown.

The Browns went 12-2 in their first
season, twice drew crowds of over 70,000,
and ended the year with a 14-9 victory over
the New York Yankees, who were the
Eastern Conference champions, for the
AAFC crown.

The next year they won 12, while losing
only one and tying one. In 1948 they were
14-0. In both years they won the championship as well. In some ways the Browns' success brought some unsatisfactory results.
They were so good that they took away
much of the excitement that a football
game can generate. Attendance throughout
the AAFC began to dip, and it even happened in Cleveland. In 1949 the Browns
drew only 189,604 (despite a 9-1-2 record
and another championship) compared to
the 399,962 that had come to the Stadium
in 1946.

The 1950 Cleveland Browns brought the sweet taste of revenge to the city. In its first year in the NFL, the team not
only won its division championship, but went on to capture the league title against the city's former Ram team.
(Cleveland Browns)

The AAFC entered discussions with the NFL, and in December, 1949 it was agreed that three of the AAFC members, the Browns, the San Francisco 49ers, and the Baltimore Colts would be accepted into the NFL for the 1950 season. The remainder of the AAFC disbanded.

The prospect of playing in the NFL was an exciting one for Cleveland fans. They had read how the Browns were taken too lightly by the NFL, their victories disparaged as resulting from playing "amateur" teams. Apparently some of that thinking also went on at NFL headquarters, for the first game assigned the Browns in 1950 was against the reigning champion Philadelphia Eagles.

The Browns began their career in the NFL on the same note that they had carried in the AAFC; they romped over the Eagles at Philadelphia 35-10 and went on to complete the season with a 10-2 record. They found themselves in a tie with the New York Giants at the end of the regular schedule, and headed for a playoff with them at the Stadium. The Browns won 8-3 with Lou Groza kicking two field goals (there also was a safety), and as American Conference champions awaited the matchup with National Conference winners, the Los Angeles Rams.

How Clevelanders savored that confrontation! It was a chance for the city to say that it was the best in professional football, and in so doing to take a measure of revenge on Dan Reeves' team. The game was played at the Stadium December 24, 1950. It is remembered as one of the most exciting championship contests of all times.

*Lou Groza (76) was a hero in the 1950 championship game. He went on to bring Browns' fans many more thrills, holding the team record for longevity with 17 years of service. He ended his career in 1967 with a total of 1,349 points on the scoreboard. Groza was inducted into the Hall of Fame in 1974.*          (The Cleveland Browns)

It was an offensive show all the way, with the Rams gaining 418 yards and the Browns 414 yards. At halftime the Rams were up 14-13. The Browns scored next, making it 20-14, but Los Angeles scored twice more in the third period for a 28-20 lead. In the final quarter Otto Graham engineered a 65-yard drive to bring the Browns within one point, 28-27. Graham was 22 for 33 and 298 yards passing, and he also ran for 99 yards during the game. With two minutes to go, the Browns marched down field. With 20 seconds left on the clock, Lou "the Toe" Groza connected on a 16-yard field goal, to give the Browns a 30-28 championship victory. The slim crowd of 29,751 who watched had braved sub-freezing temperatures and swirling snow flurries, but they witnessed a game they would long remember. The Browns and the city had established their football reputation.

Another exciting game played at the Stadium took place on November 15, 1953 against the San Francisco 49ers. It was then the largest crowd ever to see the Browns play, 80,698, and only the second time in team history that a crowd had exceeded the 80,000 figure.

In a pre-season contest at San Francisco, the Browns had beaten their old AAFC rivals 20-7. In so doing, they had sent the 49er quarterback, Y. A. Tittle, to the sidelines with an injury. When the 49ers arrived in Cleveland, they were determined to show that they could beat the Browns. It was a hard fought game, one which brought to the surface the kind of heroics that has made football so popular a sport.

In the second quarter Otto Graham, unable to find a receiver open, took off on a 19-yard run, ending up out of bounds. After he crossed the marker, however, 49er Art Michalik made contact, and his elbow opened a severe gash in Graham's mouth; he had to leave the game. Although no one subsequently blamed Michalik for deliberately injuring the quarterback, in the heat of the game the intensity of play was further increased.

Graham retired to the locker room where the team physician closed the wound with 15 stitches. The crowd thrilled when he returned to play in the second half, connecting on nine of ten passes, and bringing the Browns to a 23-21 victory. Many who witnessed the encounter report that Graham's heroics during that game represent their single most memorable moment in Municipal Stadium.

That season, for the fourth consecutive year in the NFL, the Browns captured their conference title — but for the third straight year they were defeated in the league championship game.

In 1953 the Browns were playing for new owners. Before the season began McBride had sold the team for $600,000 to a group of investors headed by Dave Jones. At that time it was the largest sum that had ever been paid for a pro football team.

In 1954 the Browns again won their conference title and this time went on to whip the Detroit Lions in the championship game at the Stadium 56-10. In 1955 they were again in the championship match and solidly defeated the Los Angeles Rams by a 38-14 score.

In each of their first six years in the NFL, the Browns had won their conference title. Compiling a 58-13-1 record, they also claimed the league title three times. Their ten-year record, including their four years in the AAFC, was even more spectacular: 105-17-4. The Browns had achieved a winning record that no team, before or since, has been able to approach.

*An exciting new era began for the Browns in 1957 when Jim Brown joined the team as a running back. During his nine years with the Browns, he rushed for a total of 12,312 yards and scored 126 touchdowns. When the Hall of Famer retired after the 1965 season, his familiar number 32 jersey was retired with him.     (Paul Tepley)*

Inevitably the days of triumph came to an end. In 1956, hampered by the loss of Otto Graham (who had retired at the end of the 1955 season), the Browns slipped to 5-7, their first losing season.

There was some benefit to that record, however, as it allowed the Browns to draft a running back from Syracuse University who was to go on to rewrite the record books and bring new excitement to the Cleveland sports scene.

Jim Brown was a rookie in 1957. In a game at the Stadium that November against the Rams, he set a new league rushing record, running for 237 yards, as the Browns won 45-31. Jim Brown added a dimension to the excitement of a football game as he was always a threat to break away for a large gain. In 1957 he helped draw 324,165 fans to the Stadium to watch the Browns, their best attendance as members of the NFL. He also helped the team get back into the championship game. Once there, however, the Detroit Lions avenged their 1954 loss by whipping the Browns 59-14 at Detroit.

The Browns continued to win over the next seasons, and Jim Brown continued to pile up the yardage, but the team was not to make it into the championship game for several more years. The Cleveland fans continued their support, however, averaging 60,000 attendance per game over the next five years.

On March 21, 1961 the Browns were sold again, this time to Arthur B. Modell, for a price which had escalated to $3,925,000. The next few years were to be trying ones for the new owner.

*Arthur B. Modell purchased the Browns in 1961. Under his leadership the team continued its winning ways, never experiencing a losing season until 1974. Modell also took over management responsibilities for the Stadium in 1973, spearheading $10,000,000 worth of improvements to the ball park. (Cleveland Browns)*

The Browns went 8-5-1 in 1961, finishing in third place in the Eastern Conference. Star running back Jim Brown at the end of the season complained publicly that he was being overworked. Quarterback Milt Plum aired his concern about a lack of enthusiasm and low player morale.

Plum found himself traded to Detroit for Jim Ninowski. The Browns then traded popular back Bobby Mitchell (who had been a star with the team since 1958) to Washington for their first draft pick of 1962 (Ernie Davis, Heisman Trophy winner and running back from Syracuse Unviersity). The fans began to grumble.

That did not prevent them, however, from supporting a new idea. Modell had announced that he would be sponsoring the first professional football doubleheader at the Stadium on August 18, 1962, as part of the pre-season schedule. Several other football owners scoffed at the idea, but the Cleveland fans did not. A crowd of 77,683, the largest ever to see a pre-season contest in Cleveland, turned out to see Detroit win over Dallas in the first game, 35-24, and the Browns win handily over the Pittsburgh Steelers in the nightcap, 33-10.

The crowd enjoyed themselves. Not only was the attendance excellent, but the fans supported the concession stands with fervor. During that one day they drank 54,000 cups of beer, 56,000 soft drinks, and 6,000 cups of coffee. They downed 66,000 hot dogs, 12,000 bags of peanuts, 4,000 boxes of popcorn, and consumed 1,800 hamburgers and 1,000 pizzas. The results of pro football's first doubleheader were clear. Modell had converted the skeptics.

*Tragedy struck the Browns in 1963. The gifted rookie, Ernie Davis (left), lost his battle against leukemia, without ever having had a chance to play in a Browns' game. Just weeks later, Don Fleming was killed in a work accident in Florida. In their memory the Browns retired their uniform numbers.     (Cleveland Browns)*

The 1962 season itself saw the Browns dip a bit further, just barely finishing over the .500 mark with a 7-6-1 record. The trade for Jim Ninowski had turned sour: the quarterback broke his collarbone, and the Browns were forced to go with back-up, Frank Ryan.

Ernie Davis, from whom so much had been expected, never had the opportunity to play. He fell ill before the season began, and tests revealed that the star running back was suffering from leukemia. He was forced to sit on the sidelines as he underwent medical treatment.

On January 9, 1963 one of the most stunning moves in Cleveland sports history took place. Art Modell announced the dismissal of head coach Paul Brown, who had led the team ever since 1946. In his 17 years at their helm, the Browns had compiled a

158-48-8 record. Perhaps because of their recent mediocre seasons and the signs of player discontent, Modell felt the time had come for a change. Unwilling to publicly criticize Brown, Modell would only say that he believed his action was "in the best interests of the Cleveland Browns." He later expressed the conviction that better lines of communication were needed for the club to achieve all that it could. In Brown's place, Blanton Collier was named the new head coach for the 1963 season.

More shock to the fans was to follow. Sixth draft choice Tom Bloom was killed in an automobile accident in early 1963. Ernie Davis succumbed to his fatal ailment on May 18. Just two weeks later the fans were stunned again when they learned that Don Fleming, a three-year veteran from Florida, had been electrocuted in a summer job accident.

*Blanton Collier was named the new head coach of the Browns for the 1963 season. The popular coach remained at the team's helm through the 1970 campaign, assembling a career won-lost record of 76-34-2.      (Cleveland Browns)*

The 1964 edition of the Browns led the fans through an exciting season. They won their conference title in the last game, and then took on the Baltimore Colts at the Stadium in the championship contest, winning 27-0 before a crowd of 79,544.      (Cleveland Browns)

It was a difficult period of time for the Browns, but the character of the team came through. Under the different style leadership of Blanton Collier, the superlative running of Jim Brown (he rushed for a record 1,863 yards that season), and the maturing arm of Frank Ryan (he threw 25 TD passes), the Browns rebounded to a 10-4 mark and missed the conference title by just one game.

The following year, 1964, was the fruition of Modell's dreams, and one that Browns' fans will not easily forget. Frank Ryan had another fine year, aided by the strong performances of receivers Paul Warfield and Gary Collins. Ernie Green and Jim Brown in the backfield provided for a balanced and powerful offense. Defense was solid too with Vince Costello, Galen Fiss, Ross Fichtner, Bill Glass, Jim Kanicki, Dick Modzelewski and colleagues. The race for the conference title was a close one, coming down to the final game of the season when the Browns had to face the Giants in New York. They swamped their challengers 52-20, and earned the right to vie for the league championship against the Baltimore Colts, to be played at the Stadium. The Browns were rated underdogs in that contest.

A crowd of 79,544 was on hand at kick-off and most of the rest of the city was listening to the game on the radio. The teams went to the locker room at halftime with no score yet on the board.

Veteran place kicker Lou Groza was the first to put some points up as he cracked a 43-yard field goal to give the Browns a second half lead 3-0. And then the Frank Ryan-Gary Collins combination went into action.

They teamed up for three touchdowns. Groza added the extra points and one more field goal as well, as the defense held the Colts to a total of 181 yards and no score! The Browns had won their fourth NFL crown 27-0. The crowd was ecstatic. That season the fans had turned out for the first time at a better than 70,000 per game average, a level that would be maintained for the next ten seasons!

The Browns were in the championship game again in 1965 against Green Bay, losing in a snowy and muddy contest, 23-12. That game was the last one for Jim Brown, who in nine years with the Browns had run for 12,312 yards and 126 touchdowns. When he retired, the Browns retired his number "32" (also retired are Graham's "14", Groza's "76", Ernie Davis' "45" and Don Fleming's "46"). Jim Brown was inducted into the Hall of Fame in 1971.

In 1967 the NFL changed its structure. Each conference was split into two divisions. Cleveland won division titles in 1967, 1968, and 1969, and went on to win the conference in each of the latter two years.

In 1968 after a slow start, the Browns won their next eight games in a row, before bowing in the final game of the season, to end with a 10-4 record. Dallas had won the other division title and arrived in Cleveland for the conference game. The Browns won it, 31-20 before a crowd of 81,497. This set up the championship game against Baltimore, to be played at the Stadium the following week. Fans were so excited that 15,000 of them stood in line in a drenching rain to buy tickets for the game.

*Paul Warfield was one of the stars in the Browns' receiving corps during the late 1960s. Here he is seen making one of his surehanded catches under typically difficult conditions.     (Paul Tepley)*

The dream of a shot at the Super Bowl (1968 was the third year for that grand finale) was not to last, however. The Baltimore Colts took revenge for their 1964 loss, this time shutting out Bill Nelsen, Leroy Kelly, Milt Morin, Paul Warfield and company by a 34-0 count. A crowd of 80,628 watched in disbelief as Cleveland native Tom Matte scored three touchdowns for the Colts, handing the Browns only the second blanking in their history.

The Browns came back in 1969, only to lose the championship game to the Vikings at Bloomington, Minnesota, by a 27-7 score.

In 1970 the merger between the National Football League and the American Football League was finalized, with the Browns (along with Pittsburgh and Baltimore) moving from the National to the American Football Conference (AFC). That year the Browns were edged from the Central Division title by the Cincinnati Bengals under the leadership of Paul Brown. In 1970, too, Blanton Collier announced his retirement after serving as head coach for eight years. The well-liked and respected coach had compiled a 76-34-2 record for the Browns.

In acknowledgement of the size of crowds that so frequently jammed the Stadium, Cleveland was honored in 1970 to host the first Monday Night Football Game, telecast across the nation. Cleveland took on the New York Jets, winning 31-21, before a crowd that met the network's highest hopes, 85,703. That figure remains the record as the Browns' all-time largest attendance.

In 1971 the Browns held their final preseason doubleheader. Popular always, the game drew 82,710 fans.

Nick Skorich was named as the Browns' new head coach for the 1971 season, and in both that year and in 1972 he led the team into the playoffs. Each time, however, the Browns bowed out of the running after first-game losses.

In 1972 a different kind of doubleheader was tried at the Stadium. Instead of two football games, this time one of the features was to be some high power entertainment. On tap for the event were singers Tony Bennett and Sarah Vaughn, with Doc Severinson and the Cleveland Orchestra. The bright skies at 5:00 p.m. that day turned dark by 7:00 p.m., and at 7:30 a violent rain storm struck the Stadium. It knocked out the $100,000 sound system set up for the event and ruined the concert. Pre-season events since that time have consisted of a football game and a giant fireworks display.

In 1973 the Browns' record dipped to 7-5-2. In 1974 they suffered their second losing season, ending with a dismal 4-10 record. Forrest Gregg became the new head coach for 1975, but the Browns remained in the cellar of their division with a 3-11 slate. In 1978 Sam Rutigliano was named the Browns' fifth head coach.

For the 1970s, the Browns' record was 72-70-2, clearly not in the same category as the 88-30-2 of the 1950s or the 92-41-5 of the 1960s. But altogether through 1979, the Browns established one of the finest overall records in the NFL — 252 victories, 141 losses, and 9 ties — for a winning percentage of .611.

Attendance figures reflected the fans' disappointment with the team's ability to keep pace with its superman style of winning in earlier years. Attendance peaked in Cleveland in 1969, when 578,360 fans watched the Browns at the Stadium. In 1975 that figure had dropped to 390,440.

*While the 1970s represented somewhat of a drought for the Browns, there were still plenty of things to cheer about. One satisfying moment for the fans came on this tackle of Pittsburgh quarterback Terry Bradshaw by the Browns' Joe Jones.   (Paul Tepley)*

*Browns' fortunes began to improve when Sam Rutigliano took over as the team's head coach in 1978. Attendance also surged upwards as the Browns began to play one exciting game after another, often winning or losing in the closing seconds of the game.   (Cleveland Browns)*

During Rutigliano's tenure, attendance has rebounded. In 1978 the Browns achieved a balanced 8-8 record. In 1979 they improved to 9-7. But more than the improvement in the actual record has been the manner in which the team either won or lost its games. More often than not, the games were decided in the last minutes — or seconds — and the team acquired a new nickname, the "Kardiac Kids." In both 1978 and 1979, attendance climbed over the 500,000 mark.

And in 1980, after an absence of eight years, the Browns once again marched to the playoffs, achieving an 11-5 record and winning the Central Division title behind the exciting quarterbacking of Brian Sipe — and they did it in true Kardiac Kid fashion.

Nine of their 16 games were decided with two minutes or less remaining on the clock, and 12 of the 16 were settled with one touchdown or less difference in the final score.

Each individual game was decided in exciting fashion, and the same held true of the 1980 season: the Browns' chances for entering the playoffs came down to the final game of the season.

The team fulfilled the city's desire for a winner, and they provided even more than that by their thrilling play and their team spirit. The city took the team to its heart and supported it fervently. The 1980 season brought a new Browns' attendance record, as 620,496 cheered on their team at the Stadium.

*Brian Sipe became the Browns' starting quarterback in 1976, and has begun to rival Otto Graham as the fans' choice for the all-time best Browns' quarterback. While Sipe is not known for his running, the record-breaking passer can scurry when necessary. Here he carries the ball to the one-yard line. (Paul Tepley)*

*The 1980 Browns captured the city's heart. The scrapping team, popularly dubbed the "Kardiac Kids," finished the season with an 11-5 mark, won their division title, and earned a playoff berth. Clevelanders set the all-time home attendance record watching them, with 620,496 passing through the Stadium turnstiles. (Cleveland Browns)*

The Browns appreciated their fans, too. When 15,000 stood in line for hours to buy tickets for the playoff game against the Oakland Raiders at the Stadium, the Browns' management saw to it that every person waiting was served hot coffee and donuts — on the house.

The playoff game followed the season's pattern. It was a day when the temperature hovered at the zero mark and the wind chill factor read -30 degrees. But the fans were there in abundance, 77,655 braving the elements on a day when the game was being televised locally. Cleveland and Oakland battled down to the wire, the game being decided in Oakland's favor 14-12; with the Browns close to the Oakland goal line, and with seconds remaining, a Sipe pass was intercepted in the end zone. The dream of the Super Bowl ended in a hushed Stadium.

As much as the Browns excited the city in 1980 and as much as they have been a highly successful team over their history, another real part of the football story in Cleveland has been the Stadium and the size of crowds it can accommodate to watch the team play. As the second largest NFL stadium (the Pontiac Silverdome is the largest, with a capacity of 80,638, compared to the Stadium's 80,385) Cleveland's lakefront park has hosted crowds of more than 80,000 on 64 different occasions. Through 1980, a total of 14,533,420 have watched the Browns in regular season play. Pre-season crowds add another 1,918,548, and for the playoffs and championship contests, another 630,972. So, altogether, since 1946, the Browns have attracted a total home gate of 17,082,940.

Cleveland Municipal Stadium has truly been not only the home of a championship organization, but the site of championship crowds as well.

*Just a few hours before game time, Cleveland Municipal Stadium is empty. Soon the players will charge out onto the field, and the roar of a packed house will greet the home team — a typical fall Sunday on the shores of Lake Erie. (Jack Muslovski)*

# CHAPTER 7

## *The Future*

Few would argue against the observation that Cleveland Municipal Stadium has more than lived up to the expectations of its proponents. As the Stadium marks its 50th anniversary in 1981, it does so with an established record of providing the community with a facility that has been useful for almost every kind of large gathering. Its utility is attested by the tens of millions of people who have visited it over the years.

But inevitably, our review of history prompts a look ahead. What is in store for the Stadium in the years to come?

Stadium watchers look about to other cities with professional baseball and football franchises and notice the number of new stadiums which have been completed in recent years. They also review the complaints that have been lodged against the Stadium at home.

Every facility has some limitations; our Stadium is no exception. For baseball, with frequent small crowds, the Stadium seems too big. For football there are times when it seems not quite large enough. There is some sensitivity to the Stadium's susceptibility to the winds off Lake Erie. These make it a chilling home for April baseball and December football.

*Spring weather for the opening of the baseball season can be chilly. Cleveland fans, however, have shown that it is really not a deterrent, as this major league record crowd for an opening day proves. A total of 74,420 turned out for this opener against Detroit in 1973.     (Cleveland Indians)*

*A plow was needed to scrape snow off the tarpaulin covering the football field in December, 1980. Bitter weather, once again, failed to discourage a sellout crowd from witnessing the Browns' playoff game against the Oakland Raiders.    (Jack Muslovski)*

So it is asked: is the Stadium's time coming to an end? Does the area require a new multi-use facility?

The question is not entirely a new one. Particularly in the 1960s, as a lack of funds kept the Stadium from being maintained properly or from a thorough modernization, there were many who felt that the time had come for a new Stadium to be built.

In 1968 Vernon Stouffer, then Chairman of the Board of the Cleveland Indians, commissioned a model for a new stadium to be crafted. He campaigned for a governmental study on the feasibility of a new park. Under the joint auspices of the City of Cleveland, Cuyahoga County, and the State of Ohio, the New York firm of Charles Luckman and Associates was commissioned to examine the possibilities. The sum of $120,000 was authorzed for the analysis.

Luckman's report was discouraging from a financial point of view. He projected that a multi-purpose stadium with a crowd capacity of 56,000, would cost $49,000,000; for a larger facility, seating 65,000, the price tag would jump to somewhat over $60,000,000 (in 1981 these cost estimates would have more than doubled). None of the sponsors felt that such expenditures were reasonably within its budgetary reach.

Attention then shifted to the possibilities of constructing a dome over the Stadium, making it a comfortable place regardless of the season. The cost estimate for this improvement came in at $44,000,000. For a city with other compelling financial needs, these studies were very disappointing.

In 1971 the Cleveland Indians' president, Nick Mileti, announced his plans to build a new arena for his basketball and hockey teams in Richfield, Ohio, some 30 miles to the south of downtown Cleveland. His Coliseum plan was based on the observation that the drawing area for such a facility could not be improved from the north (where the city is bordered by the waters of Lake Erie), but rather from the south where the population of Summit County would be attracted as easily as that of Cuyahoga County.

In 1972 Browns' president, Art Modell, bought 190 acres of land in Strongsville, a suburb to the southwest of Cleveland. He envisioned the acreage as a possible site for a new football stadium.

The construction of the Coliseum and the possible loss of the Browns from downtown Cleveland, prompted the city fathers to pursue energetically ways and means of making the Stadium a more attractive facility for its tenants.

A variety of proposals was forthcoming. One was offered by Sheldon Guren, head of U.S. Realty Investments, owners of the Terminal Tower. Another came from the firm of Christopher Associates. Osborne Engineering Company, still interested in its Stadium creation, also offered a comprehensive plan for a total redevelopment of the entire Stadium area.

Eventually, however, it was Art Modell who brought into existence the Stadium Corporation with its 25-year lease of the Stadium. With the improvements that have taken place at the Stadium under this management, thoughts of a new facility have receded into the background.

Several reasons exist for this.

*This 1960 scene at the Stadium reveals one of the facility's major assets. Its location on the Shoreway provides easy access from the east, west, and south. The Stadium is also well served by plentiful parking. (The Cleveland Press)*

First of all, most of the new stadiums built in this country have replaced older AND smaller buildings. Since Municipal Stadium has a large capacity (the largest for baseball; second largest for football), Cleveland is not faced with the necessity for creating a larger field.

Secondly, though evidence can be compiled to show a more southerly site as being demographically more attractive than the lakefront, the fact remains that the Stadium has one of the very best access systems of any major park in the country. While that fact might be doubted by the motorist caught in a traffic jam heading to or leaving from the Stadium, objective comparisons demonstrate that the Stadium's traffic situation is one of the best in the nation.

It is located on the Shoreway, connected directly with I-90 for east and west access, and to I-77 and I-71 to the south. It is just a few blocks distant from Public Square, the hub of the area's public transit network. It has parking for over 10,000 cars within lots immediately adjacent to the Stadium property.

Thirdly, there has been a renewed awareness in the Greater Cleveland community about the importance of a vital and vigorous Downtown to the well-being of the entire area. In order to attract major conventions and trade shows to the city, to lure new business, a central entertainment core is needed. Such awareness has been exemplified in the ongoing renovation of Cleveland's Playhouse Square theater complex. It has also been indicated by the recurring expressions of the need for a new indoor sports complex within the downtown area, perhaps built in conjunction with the Cleveland State University (and perhaps built adjacent to the Stadium).

Fourthly, the major objections to the Stadium — the failure to provide for its proper upkeep and renovation — have been largely answered by the improvements which have been undertaken since 1974 (and other improvements that will still be made under the terms of the lease).

Finally, it might be asked who would be willing to invest in the neighborhood of $200,000,000 to construct a new facility of similar size with the prospects of not securing a reasonable return on the investment. The nature of the stadium business is not one in which much profit is likely to result; on the contrary, most stadiums require some kind of subsidy to meet operating costs.

It would appear, then, that the future of Cleveland Municipal Stadium is secure. Improvements can be foreseen, and further lakefront development as a recreational area is near at hand.

The 1980's began with improved attendance figures for both of the Stadium's major tenants. After fifty years, the people of northeast Ohio continue to find the Stadium not only a site for exciting contemporary events, but also as a repository of many wonderful memories. The nostalgia adds to its lure.

So it would seem that millions more will continue to make their way to the Stadium, enjoy its accommodations, and put up with its limitations. It is safe to say that when the 25-year lease of the Stadium Corporation expires in 1998, Cleveland will still have a fine facility on its lakefront, in good shape and awaiting the challenges of the 21st century.

A new stadium? Who needs it? Cleveland is rightly proud to have its venerable giant on the lakefront. It has left deep footprints on the city's sands. Its stride towards tomorrow is firm.

The Cleveland Indians' mascot above Gate D has been greeting Stadium visitors for many years. It seems likely that the Indian chief will continue to smile at sports fans as the years pass by. Municipal Stadium remains secure in the affections of Greater Clevelanders.
(Jack Muslovski)

D
A
B
C

# Collect the Whole Series

If you enjoyed **Cleveland Municipal Stadium,** you will, no doubt, like the intriguing story of **The Terminal Tower Complex —** Volume I in the Cleveland Landmarks Series.

While they last, you can find the book about Cleveland's most famous landmark at many local bookstores or send $8.50, plus $0.55 tax to:

**Be Sure to Look for Future Volumes in the Cleveland Landmarks Series**

Cleveland Landmarks
  Press, Inc.
Department B
Post Office Box 9152
Cleveland, Ohio 44137